FINANCIALLY
Ever After

ALSO BY JEFF D. OPDYKE

Love & Money: A Life Guide to Financial Success

The Wall Street Journal Complete Personal Finance Guidebook

The Wall Street Journal Personal Finance Workbook

*The World is Your Oyster: The Guide to Finding Great
    Investments Around the Globe*

FINANCIALLY
Ever After

The COUPLES' GUIDE
TO MANAGING MONEY

Jeff D. Opdyke

THE WALL STREET JOURNAL.

COLLINS BUSINESS
An Imprint of HarperCollins Publishers

The Wall Street Journal® is a registered trademark of
Dow Jones and is used by permission of Dow Jones.

HarperCollins books may be purchased for educational, business, or
sales promotional use. For information please write: Special Markets
Department, HarperCollins Publishers, 10 East 53rd Street,
New York, NY 10022.

FIRST EDITION

Designed by Eric Butler

Library of Congress Cataloging-in-Publication Data

Opdyke, Jeff D.
Financially ever after : the couples' guide to managing
money / Jeff D. Opdyke. — 1st ed.
p. cm.
ISBN 978-0-06-135818-0
1. Finance, Personal. 2. Couples—Finance, Personal. I. Title.
HG179.O635 2009
332.0240086'55—dc22
2008050650

09 10 11 12 13 OV/RRD 10 9 8 7 6 5 4 3 2 1

*To Amy . . . for helping me survive the financial hiccups
we suffered in the first years of our marriage.*

CONTENTS

Section One

The Finances of Love: Money Matters *Before* Marriage

1

CHAPTER 1
TEN QUESTIONS EVERY COUPLE MUST ASK

15

Section Two

A Family Affair: Money Matters *After* Marriage

The Finances of Love

Money Matters *Before* Marriage

Who you marry matters.

Who you live with, who you commit yourself to, who you get engaged to—no matter how it is you come to bind yourself with another human being, your choice of spouse, mate, life-partner, or whatever term you arrive at, matters. To your wallet.

Crass? Possibly. True nonetheless, because the person sharing your bed will not be the person who causes the friction in your relationship; it's the person sharing your bank accounts and credit cards who will, by sheer proximity to your money, affect the financial life you live, enflame your frustrations and stymie your efforts to do with your money whatever you think is best at some particular moment.

In short, you and your partner are destined to knock heads in your marriage over financial differences neither of you could have imagined while dating. Some will be relatively small, such as a worry over a mate's bad credit history; some will be huge, such as a spouse usurping financial power in a marriage of supposed equals. No matter the size, family finance is one of the most powerful forces shaping the way partners interact—regardless of whether the partners are 20 years old and merging their lives for the first time, or 60 and working on marriage number three . . . or four.

Despite the love, the lust, the affection and the friendship, the fact is that daily life with another person is not always easy, and "love" is not always foremost in your mind when your honey fails to record the ATM withdrawals—again—leaving you to figure out why the checkbook won't balance—again. In those moments, if you just want to smack your sweetie with a sack of quarters, you're not alone. Two-thirds of newlyweds surveyed by the Association of Bridal Consultants report that conflicts over spending inflict the most damage on their marriage in the first year. Meanwhile, the Center for Marriage and Family at Omaha's Creighton University has found that debt brought into marriage ranks as one of the three most difficult hurdles new couples face during their first five years together.

Making the relationship between marriage and money all the more fitful is the fact that conflicts and disagreements aren't always about the dollars and cents but, rather, the emotions behind those dollars that dictate how each of us sees money and, in turn, how each spends and saves it. Few of us are equipped to manage that part of family finance. Though we willingly discuss privacies such as sexual exploits, even with casual acquaintances, most of us just weren't raised to talk about money. More likely, we were taught that money is one of life's most intimate affairs; it remains the last secret we dare not share, often to the point of excluding even our spouse. And all of us are infected by that longstanding bit of conventional wisdom that fighting about money is the surest path to a divorce. In truth, that's not, well, true. But more on that later.

The essence of money ultimately boils down to this:

Money in its tangible form is purely paper.
It's a tool to pay the bills, to buy life's goodies. It's dispassionate. It's logical. Its rules are easy to teach.

Money in its intangible form is purely emotion.
It's a mental state, unquestionably passionate, decidedly illogical. Its rules are so much more difficult to grasp, but necessary nonetheless if you seek to create financial harmony in your relationship.

Both of these concepts can be exceedingly difficult to implement in a marriage when you and a partner have divergent thoughts about money, its role in your life and what you want your dollars to accomplish. Too often you're missing the necessary tools that enable you to talk with one another about money without anger, frustration and hurt seeping into the conversation. You're left with essentially two choices: fight and risk making the situation worse, or shut up and risk making the situation worse. Either way, you risk making the situation worse.

The book you're holding offers a third alternative, something I'll call *family financial fluency*—the knowledge and the vocabulary that couples need to communicate effectively about their money and their feelings about money before marriage and after.

Financially Ever After is every couple's manual for managing both the real dollars and the real emotions of personal finance that course through every relationship after the "I dos" are done—and even before they're ever uttered. The goal here is to tap into those first crucial years together, a period when:

1. You're seeking to understand personal finance in the context of a family, instead of that single life you're accustomed to;

2. You're realizing you face a rash of money issues neither of you contemplated while dating (and if you did contemplate them, you recognize that you were—and likely still are—too intimidated to broach the topic without fear of a money fight);

3. You're trying to figure out how you both operate financially, how you both think about money, how you both use money and how you both communicate with one another about money.

We're going to tackle each of these topics bluntly so that you and your partner have the groundwork necessary for successfully managing both the raw dollars and cents of money, and the even rawer emotions.

And those emotions *will* arise. You will get mad, if you haven't already—and you probably already have. Your spouse will, too. You will fume. One of you will ultimately not get your way, which will end the yelling . . . and lead to the silence.

No one expects any of that, of course, before the wedding. When in love, everyone wants to believe money plays no part in marriage beyond the obvious role of funding various wants and needs. Besides, when you're talking about matters of the heart, matters of the wallet seem so trivial. Love, we all suppose, will override whatever financial disparities emerge. At the very worst, we'll just learn to grow into each other's financial quirks over time . . . right? To steal a line from the Beatles, "All you need is love."

More realistic, however, is a line from the Doobie Brothers: "What a fool believes."

Consider how happy you are right now with the love of your life— or if you're already married, think back to your pre-wedding stupor. And then consider your level of happiness when, over the course of the first year together, you realize your new spouse's highest goal is to have a good time spending every last penny you two earn on fancy dinners and fine wine, movies and plays, exquisite furnishings for an apartment in the finest zip code. And debt is accumulating on the family credit card, and those expenses that the monthly income can't handle alone are falling to your savings account, which is growing ever more anemic with each passing month. Or, to be fair about it, think about your level of happiness if your love's highest and best use for money is stashing every available dollar in a savings or investment account, sapping the family's ability to enjoy some of the pleasures that life offers up.

Who you committed yourself to matters.

Of course, most folks don't envision such frustrations when they're in love and talking about promising their lives to one another, whether through marriage or some other union. So many more pressing matters consume your mental energy that money easily slips to the bottom of your list. And besides, money seems fairly simple: You make some; you save some; you spend some. Not much to worry about, really.

Only, money rarely works that way. You never seem to make enough. You never seem to save enough. You always seem to spend too much. And you are forever trying to find a better balance among all three. Then, you go off and partner up with someone, and just like that you've doubled your problems. Because now, it's not just how much money you earn and save and spend—it's that, times two.

As such, the financial partnership that is a big part of any marriage can be a never-ending source of conflict, stress, anger, frustration, and resentment. Sometimes those emotions will seethe beneath the surface for years, gnawing at the foundations of love. Sometimes they will explode into the open the moment they arise. Sometimes financial differences are enough to cleave a couple apart. Sometimes you'll stay together till the end, yet never really achieve the kind of happiness you once imagined you'd find in building a life together.

Whatever the case, managing money within the framework of a relationship can be one of the most challenging chores any couple must confront on a daily basis. The reason: The fights, arguments and disagreements about money are rarely about money. They are, instead, internalized struggles centered on power, independence, self-esteem, security, control—a wide range of underlying emotions that are tough to pinpoint, much less talk about, and so they find other ways of rising up to make themselves known. Money is frequently the conduit because it is so easy to argue about. Money is central to our lives and is a common denominator we think we understand. By the time we're old enough to pair off, we've been handling money in some manner for at least two decades, often more, during which time we've formed our own opinions on how our money is best utilized. When a partner breaches one of our personal financial pillars—no matter how negligible the breach—we use that as a springboard to unleash pent-up emotions often tied to something entirely different. Maybe your lover barks at you one evening for taking money out of the bank without recording the transaction, and you explode into a rage. That fight isn't about forgetting to record the ATM withdrawal; it's about your underlying hatred of being micromanaged and your anger over your partner's iron-fisted control of the family's pocketbook. But you can't fight about any of that because . . . well, because you don't know how to fight about any of that. You don't even know where to begin that discussion. And your partner, meanwhile, feels the need to micromanage because that's the family dynamic your partner saw growing up and, so, is simply repeating history as an adult.

Ahhh, the simplicity of money.

None of this matters, of course, until after you're living under the same roof. Until that point, you're free to do with your money whatever you wish, and no one has the right to question your actions— though, of course, your partner might snipe at you on occasion for spending too much or not saving enough, or being a penny-pincher.

But once you're together in the same household . . . well, that alters the equation entirely. By sheer proximity, each partner's financial idiosyncrasies and money habits necessarily impacts the other. That's the genesis of the money fights that emerge. Suddenly, you're around each other continually and you can't help but begin noticing, even on the periphery, the way money courses through the relationship—the words used to describe money matters or invoked during a financial fight; how bills are handled and credit cards employed; how cash is disbursed, spent or horded; how you two disagree about certain financial issues, even if you don't talk about any of them.

This proximity might arise because you've gotten engaged and agreed to move in with your future spouse. It could be you two never want to marry, but have committed yourselves to each other and will build a life together. You could be in a new marriage or one that's already a couple years old. Whatever the case, when you commit yourself emotionally to another person and agree to become a family, then you are, by definition, committing yourself financially. Not only are you merging lives, you're merging your pocketbooks. That's rarely a smooth transition, and it's never romantic.

I promise, love might have myriad powers, but your views on spending and saving are fundamental to your DNA. Same with your partner. As such, even the most compatible couples are destined to butt heads financially.

Moreover, don't presume that money matters won't matter until a marriage certificate binds you two legally. Relationships don't all unfold along neat, clean marital lines. Finances affect every relationship to some degree, no matter how that relationship is structured. Some of the worst financial disasters happen to people who are not married—people who are in love and begin to entangle their money and assets in complicated ways without the proper legal structure.

Let me demonstrate my point by stretching an example to a ridiculous—though certainly not impossible—length. I'll be the guy for a minute, and you be the girl. . . . We're so in love. We've been dating for a few years and we live together. The diamond on your finger is proof that I'm committed to you, and the wedding is next year, a nice little chapel overlooking the ocean and that honeymoon on Thai beaches we've always talked about. You know, let's just go ahead and merge our accounts now. That way there's only one checkbook to balance, just one credit card statement to pay every month. We've already merged everything else in our life, so let's just go all the way.

And you—remember, you're playing the girl—are so in love with the idea that I'm so into building a life together that you agree. And you roll your $5,000 into the joint checking or savings account. And there we are, a happy little couple on our way to a beautiful existence.

Only, there's this little secret I never told you about. Actually, I met a Thai flight attendant on my last trip to Asia, and I really dig her. I've decided I don't think I actually want to marry you and honeymoon in Thailand so much as I want to be with this girl in Thailand. So I'm moving. Oh, and I need some cash to live on while I'm there, and I knew you'd probably have a small conniption fit about this and say "No!" if I asked for the money, so yesterday I emptied the checking account because it was a joint account and, technically speaking, that makes it "our" money, so the bank let me withdraw it with no questions asked. Really, sweetie, it's been a fun few years, but I'm going now. I'll be sure to drop you a postcard from Koh Samui—I know you really wanted to see the beaches there.

And the worst part for you is that the rent is due in three days and the American Express bill arrived in the mail that afternoon, and here you are with no money to your name because the person you were so in love with is gone with your cash.

That might seem contrived, but some variation of this type of financial and emotional disaster routinely occurs when you merge your finances outside of marriage. Yes, you can prove you put the money in the account and that it is, therefore, your money. But that doesn't negate the fact that you willingly deposited the money in a joint account that, by law, gave each of you equal, unfettered access to the dollars. And if your wonderful fiancé absconds with the money, well, then it's up to you to try to hunt him down and reclaim it—assuming he hasn't spent it all on travel, fun and games.

That leads to the Cardinal Rule of Love and Money:

Never join your finances outside of marriage.

There are bad financial decisions, and then there are horrendously bad financial decisions. Merging your finances before there is a legal union binding you together can be magnitudes worse than even the most horrendous financial decisions.

When you merge finances, you are in effect giving away your money while at the same time taking on whatever financial warts come packaged with your partner. A joint checking, savings or investment account gives me—your devoted lover—free rein to raid it whenever I want without seeking your permission or signature. If our relationship fails and I wander off with the bulk of your money, there's little you can do about it. If I sell off all the blue-chip stocks you put into our joint brokerage account so that I can take a flyer on a hot tip I heard about at the barbershop—a hot tip that turns out colder than a Siberian winter—there's nothing you can do to recoup the losses I accumulated.

And then there's the nightmare of joint credit cards. When you apply for credit jointly, you are, by law, agreeing that both of you will be responsible for whatever legitimate charges appear on the bill. Let me repeat the three key words: Both. Of. You.

This means you are legally responsible for whatever charges your partner amasses, regardless of whether you knew about the purchases. Credit card companies do not care that you didn't actually sign for that $25,000 Harley motorbike, or the $25,000 wardrobe from Barneys New York. Nor do they care that your lover has now dumped you, run off to Singapore with a new lover, and refuses to pay the bill. They care singularly about one small, legally relevant fact: You signed an application agreeing to repay all legitimate charges—and those massive charges your partner accumulated are considered legitimate, since your partner is a co-owner on the account. That leaves you liable for at least half the money owed, possibly more.

When you're the victim of these sorts of catastrophes, you're left wondering how this could have happened and why you didn't see it coming. The answer is easy: Love blinds us all to the financial evil that lurks inside a heart. You only see it after the fact, after something has gone terribly wrong. Certainly, the vast lot of people you might end up with in a relationship are not out to destroy your life financially. Most are just trying to build a happy life with you. But along the way good but misguided intentions can lead to world of financial hurt. In the worst cases, that hurt can lead to the dissolution of a relationship and the loss of love, not to mention money. That's why it's important to understand as much as you can about your partner financially.

That, then, is where we start this book: Developing the skills you need to succeed financially in your relationship. It all begins with a series of ten questions that, whether you're living together, engaged or already married, you need to resolve in some fashion. I'm not saying you necessarily need to sit down with your partner and start firing off these questions, demanding answers *now*. That won't work. In some cases, you may not necessarily even need to ask the question; you might already know the answer, or you'll come to it on your own through observations and normal, daily conversations. In other instances, you will have to ask. None of this will be romantic. Then again, there's nothing particularly romantic about a relationship plagued by financial quarrels or one that ends horridly because neither of you cared to consider the ways that dollars and emotions flow through your finances.

The best moment to begin talking seriously about these ten questions is the moment the relationship moves toward a certain permanency. Maybe that's when talk of engagement and marriage arises, or it could be earlier, when you two decide it's time to live together. His and hers finances grow intertwined at that point, and, as such, you're free to ask the hard questions since both of your financial decisions will have impacts on the relationship in some fashion.

This doesn't imply that you should stay mum about money until you're on the road to living together. Once you've been dating long enough to both know that you're really a couple and not just two singles hooking up for fun and games, it's fine to ask financial questions. And, as you'll see, sometimes you don't even need to ask a question. Everyday observations, once you begin to catalog them, will start to reveal some of what you need or want to know.

Curious how your partner manages debt, or deals with financial stress? Take note of how often the credit card comes out and the size of the purchases for which it's used. You'll learn a lot about how this person views credit without ever asking. Listen for complaints about bills or creditors calling, telltale signs that money is a stressful subject and that your mate has issues over hewing to a budget, earning up to his or her potential or struggling with self-restraint when it comes to controlling immediate wants. Instincts are powerful detectives; over time they clue you in to a lot that you don't immediately recognize. Early on you might love the oceanfront condo your partner owns, but months into the relationship you might begin to suspect that the home is really more than your partner can afford . . . and so is the sports car . . . and that gorgeous wardrobe . . . and the quarterly getaways to the Caribbean. After a while, your instincts are adding up all these facts, and you see a picture emerging of someone living too well on the back of American Express and Visa.

Not all financial observations are so negative, of course. Financial confidence and security shine through, too. You hear it in talk of planning for the future and an absence of fretting about bills in the present. You sense it when your partner talks of having to run to a meeting with a financial advisor, or mentions investments in stocks and bonds and real estate. You see it in the day's mail sitting on the counter, envelopes from the household names of personal finance—Fidelity, Charles Schwab, and Morgan Stanley. These are signs of someone who is, if not financially savvy, at least astute enough to be saving and investing for the future.

Just remember that at the end of the day, it's not the money that's at the root of money fights. *It's the inability to communicate effectively about money.* If you can learn to talk about your family's finances instead of keeping your concerns and frustrations bottled up—and these upcoming questions will help you begin to make strides in that direction—you will find effective, productive ways to find common ground.

You will find the ways to make each other happy financially.

CHAPTER 1

TEN QUESTIONS EVERY COUPLE MUST ASK

QUESTION 1: *Do You Have a Basic Understanding of Money?*

This seems like a no-brainer. Just about everyone has been handling cash in some fashion since grade school—of course you have a basic understanding of money.

Only, many people don't.

If they did, then why does research out of Indiana State University find that young adults—those between 20 and 24—represent the fastest-growing source of bankruptcy filings in the country? Meanwhile, the Gen-X crowd—those born generally between 1965 and 1978—is more likely to file for bankruptcy than were their Baby Boomer parents at the same age. Those bankruptcies are sparked in large part by soaring credit card debt and the fact that too many homeowners opt for magical mortgages that open the door to a house well beyond their ability to pay. This led to a rash of foreclosures that has pushed people out of their homes, often robbing them of whatever equity they had in their house.

None of that indicates a basic understanding of money. It does, however, indicate a basic understanding of spending—and that's the problem. Fact is, Americans in general—not just Gen-Xers—are a financially illiterate lot for the most part. Studies of everyone from high school seniors up through older adults routinely bear this out. As a society, we spend more than we save so that our savings rate as a nation is among the lowest in the world.

You can see why it is important for spouses to know if their partners possess basic money knowledge. The wiser you each are financially, the smarter the decisions you'll make together, ultimately leading to a more fulfilling relationship, since you'll both feel more secure financially and will more likely achieve whatever it is you want your money to achieve.

But here's the rub: Financial prowess does not reside in everyone, nor does it appeal to everyone. Lots of folks aren't naturally inclined to care about the minutiae of money: managing investments, comparing insurance policies, or shopping for the best interest rates on savings accounts and mortgages. That's enough to cause a conflict right there. The one who does care will ultimately be frustrated that their partner could care less; and the one who could care less will ultimately be frustrated by the seemingly constant—incessant— focus on money. It can be a never-ending spiral that intensifies as you slip deeper into the vortex. The money-conscious partner tries ever harder to instill financial values into a partner; the partner tries ever harder to rebuff those efforts—all of which leads to an even harder push on both sides. At some point, your conflict erupts into discord that flows through other parts of the relationship, and even into the bedroom.

I'm not saying that to succeed in marriage you must absolutely master the intricacies of personal finance and be able to wax philosophically on the debate between growth and value stocks or the merits of fixed-rate versus adjustable-rate mortgages. If you know all that stuff, great. If you care to know all that stuff and you don't, pick up any one of the numerous comprehensive personal-finance guidebooks (I'm partial to *The Wall Street Journal Complete Personal Finance Guidebook* and companion workbook . . . but, then again, I wrote those).

The real problem you must address—the problem Question 1 is getting at—is what to do when neither of you, or only one of you, really understands money. That must be rectified, otherwise you're likely to spend your relationship continually insecure financially, or frustrated with each other, or maybe even routinely fighting.

You probably already know if you have a good understanding of money. If you regularly balance your checkbook when the statement arrives, if you live below your means so that you can afford to contribute to your 401(k) plan every paycheck or an IRA every year, if you refuse to carry a balance on your credit card, and if you're leery of—not excited by—an interest-only mortgage that allows you to buy the $300,000 house you otherwise can't afford with a traditional mortgage, then you probably have as solid a financial foundation as you need to grow your wealth. If none of that rings true to you—or if you sense that none of this defines your partner—there's a gap in the financial knowledge base you need to confront.

You don't necessarily have to ask if your partner understands money—your partner may not even know how to answer that question. But you will hear the answer in comments about late fees imposed on a credit card again, grousing about never having the money to afford the car-insurance premium when it routinely rolls around, gripes about an inability to make ends meet. Ask simple questions like "Do you have money saved in your 401(k) plan?" and listen for the "why" behind the yes or no answer. Ask whether your partner follows a budget, then ask why. What kind of car does the love of your life drive? Or what about the house, the furnishings, the style clothes hanging in the closet? Does the house itself, or the neighborhood it's located in, seem consistent with what you generally gauge to be this person's level of income? Do the furnishings and the clothes square up as well? All of these offer snippets of information you can use to answer Question 1.

Recognize, though, that some of the financial gap you see might have emotional roots. I talk to lots of couples in my job as a personal-finance writer and columnist, and after all these years I'm still astounded at the degree to which people will open up to me—a stranger they've never met—about their financial lives. Though the details are different, many of the stories are the same: "My (husband/wife/partner, fill in the blank) and I have very different styles and we fight about money because (he/she) doesn't understand me."

Chances are you'll never convince your partner to see things your way. Money traits are part of our DNA, instilled in us by our parents and our experiences with money growing up. Few people recognize this fact when they're adults, assuming that they can either be who they are in a relationship, for better or worse, or that they can change their partner to fit their own financial style. That's just not going to happen for the most part.

So here's how you deal with it: Seek help.

If you're the person who has money skills, but your partner doesn't, you're probably convinced that if your partner would just pay attention to what you can teach, they'd learn so much from you, and then your combined financial life would be so much more fulfilling. But here's what your partner is thinking when you start talking money: "Please shut up dear god not again I can't believe we're talking about money again when I have so many other things to worry about hell it's only money get a life why do you always harp on me about money I don't care about money just leave me alone and shut up already!" And, if you're the person who doesn't care, here's what your partner is thinking: "Why are you so blind to what you're doing don't you see that you're screwing us financially because you continue doing the same stupid things financially and I'm busting my butt to help you understand that our life could be so much better and secure financially but talking to you about this is like talking to a geranium what's your problem money is important to our future together!"

What you need to break through this inability to communicate is a neutral person, such as a financial planner, in particular a fee-only planner who won't try to sell you a bunch of products and services. You'll just be paying for the planner's time that you consume, the most efficient way to buy financial advice.

If neither of you is a financial savant, a planner will help you both cut through to the financial issues that are most important to daily living and planning for the future, and get you both working toward common goals. This way, you're not running off in the wrong direction, carping at each other about issues that aren't necessarily that important. Planners can help you fashion a budget that takes into account each of your financial needs, yet still has you saving something for your future. This speeds up the learning curve and puts you both on solid, financial footing together.

In situations where you're financially savvy and your partner isn't, consider buying your partner the gift of a few hours with a fee-only planner. Call ahead and emphasize to the planner some of the concerns you have and some of the issues specific to your relationship that you'd like covered. This way, your partner gains a basic understanding of money in an environment that's not as tense as it can be at home with you playing financial drill sergeant. If money matters are a constant struggle, consider regularly visiting a planner together, or maybe even keep one on retainer, so that you and your partner can pop in for advice on whatever financial issues arise. With such a strategy, you're letting the planner absorb the energy that would otherwise fuel a fight, and you're getting impartial advice that can work to bridge the differences separating you two.

And if you're the weak link financially in the relationship, or you just don't care about money to begin with, investing a few hours in a financial planner will at least help you begin to understand why your partner is so concerned about saving that $4,000 in an IRA instead of spending it on the vacation to Jamaica you want. That doesn't mean a planner will talk you out of your consumer wants and side with your partner's investment wants. It means, instead, that the planner can provide you the tools to argue your side of the debate from a more logical perspective, rather than spewing the emotion that your partner doesn't understand. It may be that the planner shows you how to afford both expenses or suggests a compromise that suits you both. The point is that you don't have to care about the money, you just have to care enough about the relationship to at least want to understand where your partner is coming from so that together you can forge a path that meets both sets of needs.

QUESTION 2:
What Is Your Money History?

Admittedly, this question is squishy. And it's likely to shape up as one of the more difficult questions to answer. Still, how you were raised in terms of money has shaped in many ways who each of you are today, financially speaking, though few people instinctively recognize that.

Think about it, though: What you experienced as a kid is etched in your memory banks—everything from how your parents paid the bills, to how they talked about money (or didn't talk . . . or screamed), to how they spent and saved and complained about the family's finances or the new cars the neighbors seemed to buy every year. Maybe you're a women who saw your mom as a financial weakling, subservient to a husband who imposed his will over the checkbook, and as such you now vow to always maintain your own account regardless of what your partner says. Maybe your mom or dad taught you the ins and outs of managing money effectively, and now, as an adult, you don't struggle financially nor do you worry about money, confident in your skills to balance your saving and spending.

Your experiences have determined who you are. These are the roots of your financial behavior. By the same measure, your partner has experiences as well. And problems arise because who you are isn't always compatible financially with that person on the other side of the bed.

Let's illustrate this with a rather extreme example: The son of Richie Rich hooks up with the daughter of Ebenezer Scrooge. While extreme in terms of personalities, this scenario is all too common in relationships and a classic cause of discord. Richie's son, the spender, we'll call him Buck, is destined to spend and likely will rebel when Scrooge's daughter, the saver, we'll call her Penny, tries to impose financial discipline over the checkbook and credit cards. Penny, meanwhile, is compelled to save, and is equally likely to spin into a frenzy as Buck cavalierly (at least in Penny's eyes) throws around the family's money. Neither realizes that their actions and reactions stem from the individual financial histories that no one pays much attention to.

In a relationship, you might assume your spouse has no real interest in the family's money because no questions are ever asked. So, you blithely go about your normal routine spending and saving the way you want to under mistaken assumptions that your partner doesn't care. Yet the real reason behind this lack of inquisitiveness has nothing to do with disinterest and everything to do with the fact—which you don't know about—that your sweetheart grew up in a family where money was never, ever discussed. Unbeknownst to you, your spouse simply never learned to talk about money because Mom and Dad never asked questions and neither volunteered information to the other. So, your partner just assumes it's improper to raise the topic— though inside rages a person screaming to ask many questions about the way you're handling the bills and investments.

As such, some of the financial angst in a relationship can be avoided by simply talking about what you each remember of your financial education and experiences, and what you remember about your parents' money habits. From this each of you gains a bit of historical context that explains how the other operates financially and why. And you might just surprise yourself to realize you're expressing as an adult many of your parents' money habits, be they good or bad.

The easiest way into this discussion is to ask:

What does money represent to you?

Maybe that answer is security; the more money in the bank, the greater the feeling of financial staying power in the event bad things happen. Maybe that answer means choices, the ability to pick selectively among a menu of financial wants instead of being shoehorned into something you don't necessarily want because it's all you can afford. Maybe the answer is lifestyle, where money offers the opportunity to live how you want, with the cars and houses and clothes and such that appeal to you, even if beyond your immediate means. Maybe it's time together on family vacations twice a year, providing a child with a private-school education, or the means to care for aging parents one day. Maybe it means power and prestige, attained through long hours propelling yourself ever higher through the corporate ranks.

No matter the answer, the words begin to frame you and your partner's individual financial values, and ultimately shape the issues you'll need to discuss. If you hear "money means I can buy what I want," dig into that. Does that mean a partner would rather have fun, spending every free dime today, than worry about tomorrow? Does that mean parents were too controlling and your partner really isn't a shopaholic but would be happiest with a spouse who doesn't exert financial primacy? Does your financial temperament mesh with that?

Don't consider any answer a deal breaker; the question isn't designed to solicit that answer. Instead, examine the answers to gauge where your values merge and diverge. In those divergences you'll find the most important information. Because while similar values are nice, and they certainly serve to strengthen a marriage, they're not going to ultimately divide you. The friction, frustrations and fights lurk in those divergences. This is where you must concentrate your energy fashioning the compromises you both can live with.

Let's use another simple example: You're the spender, your partner's the saver. Recognize that that's who you each are, for better or worse (and dogmatic savers can be just as difficult as unrepentant spenders), and from there learn to work together to make each other content. That might mean the spender agrees not to spend more than a certain dollar amount or percentage of the family's income each month, while the saver agrees to dial back what the spender sees as an overly militant savings regimen. That gives the spender the joy of feeling like a paycheck is affording a fulfilling life, while the saver feels a sense of security and accomplishment as the family's war chest grows larger with each payday. That's the art of compromise—the art of managing a relationship.

Whatever you do, do not belittle each other's financial wants, needs or expectations. That, I promise, will lead to deeper resentments and ultimately subvert your efforts. Everyone is different, and just because you despise the color fuschia doesn't mean it's not a gorgeous shade for which someone else might have a passion. Accept the differences for what they are—unavoidable, expected, the reality of life—and seek common ground together.

The thing to be aware of with money histories is that, in some instances, they hide chronic problems that lead to, or stem from, pathological disorders. All of us are planted somewhere along a financial continuum that stretches between pathological spending to pathological savings—and neither of those extremes is healthy. Our individual placement is defined by how we think about and use our money. In the middle is the healthy median, where money flows through life

with ease, where we are confident in ourselves as the resource responsible for our own success and security, rather than seeing money as
the source. We control the money; it's an internal thing.

Move in either direction from that median, however, and increasing degrees of emotional stress take hold, leading up to pathological
disorders in which people are unable to control their spending, to the
point that they spend themselves into bankruptcy, or must save com-
pulsively, sometimes to the point of avoiding expenses necessary for
their own security or the security of their family. In both instances,
money and what it provides is the only source of comfort. *Money* controls us; it's an external thing.

Managing such pathologies generally requires professional assistance. So if you fear—or know—you fit into this category, it's best
to find a counselor who can help address the underlying issues effectively. If you suspect a partner has a pathological money disorder,
don't just throw out over dinner that you think professional help is in
order. That won't sit well—at all. Instead, suggest that you both talk
to a financial professional to help the two of you deal with the money
concerns that are undermining the relationship. Arrange a meeting
with a financial counselor—sort of a marriage counselor whose specialty is financial matters—and call ahead to explain your problems.
Through questioning, the counselor will pick up on any concerns and
suggest where to find necessary help.

To be clear: Just because one of you is a spender and the other a
saver, it doesn't mean that you're on a destructive path to a meltdown.
It just means you're two normal people who happen to see money
from different perspectives. There's nothing abnormal about that. It
does mean, however, that you both have some talking to do about
your money histories so that you can understand each other better
and, together, narrow whatever divide exists.

QUESTION 3:
What Are Your Financial Aspirations?

Not every conversation about money must be intense to be effective. This is one that's not. This is the fun talk—generally speaking.

Simply put, what are your hopes and dreams for yourself and your family? The college you want your kids to attend—or whether you even want kids. The lake house you someday hope to own. The vacations you want to take. The classic Corvette you want to restore. Saving enough to retire early to a sailboat in the Caribbean . . . or a bass boat on a Tennessee lake. Or maybe you see yourself moving out of the corporate world and into that bakery or bistro or winery you've always wanted to own, or signing up to do pro bono work for a charitable organization.

Whatever dream you have, no matter how big or small—no matter how ridiculous, silly or unattainable you think it is—now is the time to mention it. This is where you begin to lay out the path you want to follow in life, and you begin to see the path your partner expects to follow. More important, you begin to see where these two paths potentially diverge in meaningful, relationship-altering ways.

An easy way to address this question: Make a game of it. Spend a few minutes each jotting down on a sheet of paper, or even the back of a napkin if you're out at an eatery, whatever wants and dreams and desires you have for your own life. Then, take turns sharing the items on your list. Talk about each one, explain its importance to you, provide the necessary context for understanding why it made the list. Call this your "Accomplishments Before I Die List," or whatever you think it should be named. You might find some overlapping dreams. That's good; it gives you immediate, shared goals to pursue together. Many dreams might be far apart. But that's OK; for now this is just a get-to-know-you-better exercise.

Go into this discussion recognizing that you may never attain all the dreams you scribble down. That's fine . . . and largely irrelevant. This conversation isn't about how you're going to get everything you want in life. It aims simply to help you articulate your individual life and financial priorities so that you both know what the other will expect from the resources you earn together. In answering this question, you're highlighting where common ground already exists and where you need to look for opportunities to pull in the same direction.

Don't trash your lists. Save them. They are effectively the roadmap you're going to pursue together in your relationship—in essence, your scorecard. Keep it safe through the years, and return to it periodically to re-examine where you are, what you've accomplished and which items on the list need to change—and see if any need to be added—because your desires have changed. That will help you gauge whether your actions match your words. So, for instance, if both of you agree that a key family goal is saving enough to fund your child's education costs completely, you will surely recognize that you're not living up to your dreams if you're buying the big house outside your price range, adding the swimming pool with a home-equity loan, and leasing a new Porsche instead of buying an affordable Honda.

Now, I said this is the fun talk, however this question—what are your financial aspirations?—also helps clarify the stumbling blocks that could derail "and they lived happily every after."

Within each person's financial aspirations are, potentially, the seeds of strife that you must take note of. You might hear "I want to be able to afford my alma mater for my child," or "I want to one day return to my hometown and buy a house near my parents." Real problems can come from such dreams when they clash. And here's how that might happen: Wanting to pay for college implies one of you absolutely wants kids, but what if the other most assuredly does not? That's a problem fundamental to the very basis of your relationship's foundation. Wanting to return to your hometown is fine, but what if one of you is pursuing a career path that means an ex-patriot's life in Europe or Asia? That's another fundamental problem.

Such problems exert pressure on the relationship, particularly if a dream emerges unexpectedly. Imagine the reaction if you were to come home and excitedly announce "I'm up for a job in Hong Kong! I have always wanted to live and work in Asia. We're going to have so much fun!" Don't be surprised if your partner—who has never heard of this dream and who might already be building a career here in the states—isn't bouncing off the ceiling with you. Such surprise dreams don't always go over as well as you might hope.

Use this third question, then, not only to frame a discussion about your individual wants in life, but to understand where competing dreams flag potentially serious conflicts ahead. Spotting those conflicts early gives you the time necessary to effectively fashion a compromise that keeps you both happy, or provides the clarity to determine that ultimately this is not the relationship for you in the long term.

QUESTION 4:
What Are Your Career Expectations?

Few new couples—outside of possibly those in the military—realize the degree to which a career can potentially impact a relationship.

I touched on one small example in the previous question, the idea that one of you wants an ex-pat's life while the other is more concerned with moving home. Only a small sliver of couples will ever face a career decision that dramatic. More likely are the more mundane choices couples confront routinely. Do you assume, for instance, that you and your spouse will both work full time throughout your relationship, each climbing the corporate ladder to greater salaries?

Does one of you expect to become a stay-at-home parent and that the family will live off one income after a child is born?

Both of you might be OK with the ultimate answers. But here's why you need to address this question early on: Both of you might *not* be OK with the answers. The day could well arrive when one of you says to the other, "But I thought we were both going to keep working to pay for all these things we want in life!" And the other replies with, "But I thought you knew I've always wanted to stay home with the kids!"

Career defines a huge piece of our lives. It is, to a large degree, who we are. Think about it: The first question most people ask a new acquaintance is, "So, what do you do for a living?" Moreover, the paychecks we earn fund the expectations and dreams we pursue. As such, this is a question you need to ask each other outright. You don't want to assume you know the answer based on observations or little things you hear here and there, because a wrong assumption can come back to bite you hard later in life.

When it comes to this particular question, there is no one right answer that applies to every couple. Each relationship has its own dynamics that will determine the best course. No matter the situation, though, success mandates some kind of compromise . . . assuming, of course, that each other's expectations are clashing.

Imagine the angst that surfaces if you decide to leave the workforce to raise children, and your partner, who has never been made aware of this desire, blows a gasket over the sizable reduction in the family's income. Not to be overly sexist, but in most of these situations it's the guy who pushes vigorously for the woman to maintain her employment, worried that the loss of income and increased costs of raising a child will hamper the family's ability to save adequately for the future, afford new cars or even go on annual vacations. Worse, at the very moment the family needs a bigger, more expensive place to live, the family's paycheck is shrinking. Little surprise such news can stoke a heated argument.

Or consider the conflict that can emerge when you both earn promotions at the same time—to different cities. Whose career takes precedence? What if your job promotes you to a different city, but your partner has no desire to leave a great job, is unwilling to start all over again, and doesn't want to lose seniority and maybe a year or two of contributions to a company retirement plan? Or what if you're that person who doesn't want to forsake your career for a partner who wants to move for his or her career? Again, whose career wins?

Navigating these career issues require that you spend time discussing what expectations you each bring to the relationship. That gives both of you the opportunity to share your views and, over time, shape your future together long before career choices are an issue. It gives you time to formulate the compromises necessary to success. So let's take that example where she wants to leave the workforce after the kids arrive, and he's freaked out by the prospect of a slimmer level of income. This is a frequent source of tension among couples and the cause of many a fight ostensibly about money, but just as often about an underlying emotional struggle: He wants a sense of financial security for the family, she wants to provide the same nurturing environment she knew growing up with a stay-at-home mom.

Those arguments, both legitimate, naturally grind against one another because they're routinely framed in black-and-white terms, an either/or debate that puts both partners on edge and in a defensive posture verbally, trying to convince one another—or strong-arm each other—to change their view.

This is where the art of the compromise comes in. Doesn't it make more sense to find a solution that makes everyone feel their concerns have been heard and addressed satisfactorily, rather then one of you getting your way by sheer force of will? That's just the sort of solution that creates underlying and long-held frustrations that accumulate over time. During your relationship, you may never hear about this event ever again, but then amid yet another money fight your partner, in a fit of anger, exclaims, "You always want it your way! What about what I want?" And you might play dumb and say something defensive like, "What are you talking about?" And what your partner is talking about is this instance, from years earlier, when instead of looking for the compromise, you hewed only to what you wanted.

Search, and you will find a workable solution together. It may not come to you immediately; you both might need some time to think about it or some time to consider the suggestions you offer to one another. In this particular situation—the stay-at-home/stay-at-work debate—maybe the parent who wants to stay at home finds a way to create freelance income working just a few hours a day when the baby is napping, and promises to return to work in some fashion once a child is in school full time. The parent who wants a partner to remain in the workforce might agree to reconfigure the family's finances to accommodate the reduced income. That might mean scaling back the caliber of vacation so that more money can flow into savings, or it might mean earmarking less for savings if you still want to afford the meals out every week. The point is these are decisions you make together. You can't impose your career wants over the relationship.

I promise that such conversations will not always be easy—in fact, they could be quite tense at times. When career expectations clash, they bring to the surface all sorts of issues about financial security, power and the ability to pursue life's niceties, which might be far more crucial to one spouse's happiness than it is to the other's. Don't let that stop you from asking this question, though. You both need to know the answer. As a couple, you cannot go blindly into a relationship just expecting the career stuff to work itself out along the way. While it very well might—and, if so, call it a lucky happenstance—it also very well might explode when partners' assumptions do not match. And now here you are fighting about whose priorities take precedence.

QUESTION 5: *What Are Your Financial Assets and Liabilities?*

No one wants to ask—or answer—this question.

Money is such a taboo topic early in a relationship that people are disinclined to share information on how much money they earn, how much they've saved and how much debt they've accumulated on credit cards, car loans, auto leases, mortgages and even school loans. The very question can send so many wrong messages.

Nevertheless, this is one of the most important questions couples can ask. After all, how much money you have and how much money you owe will define so much of your life together.

Money in the bank represents financial security, a source of income and a resource to help afford the items that will make your life more enjoyable or more comfortable. Debt, meanwhile, is often a source of angst, and it's assuredly an expense that will necessarily drain part—possibly a significant part—of your family's monthly income. Moreover, debt can ultimately prevent you (the both of you) from pursuing what you want individually and as a couple, since the money you otherwise would tap for a new house, a car, a TV, a vacation, whatever, is, instead, earmarked for some creditor.

Therefore, knowing the assets and liabilities each of you will bring into the relationship is paramount. It's a basic building block for so much of your financial life. And don't think this information is easily hidden, particularly in a marriage. Unless you have an offshore bank account or wads of cash stuffed into a secret safe-deposit box that you will continue to hide from your spouse in marriage—and, really, not such a wise decision—assets and liabilities will make themselves known in some fashion.

The assets you have, for instance, will generate some level of income and the IRS just loves to know about "some level of income" every year. Moreover, your partner is destined to see account statements arrive in the mail or, if you're married, see your tax returns at some point and question what these accounts are and the origin of this non-wage income. You can try to lie about it or make up some excuse, but that's just going to elevate the suspicions, begin to erode the trust and spark another set of questions that you'll have to figure out how to evade as well. Not a good circle to trap yourself in.

Meanwhile, any undisclosed debt or secret credit card accounts won't stay hidden forever. These accounts are uncovered in due time through applications for loans or mortgages you pursue as a couple, and certainly when your partner asks to look at your credit report from time to time—as any financially smart partner will request, no matter how deep the trust and love.

Atrocious debt emerges when you two apply for, say, a home loan jointly. Mortgage companies review the credit history for both buyers on the application. Two possibilities result: The lender rejects the application altogether or, more likely, offers a higher interest rate that, in turn, means more money draining out of the family's monthly income. Either way, the spouse with excellent credit will certainly wonder why (and that's because people with excellent credit generally know they have excellent credit and know they should receive a favorable interest rate). Again, two possibilities arise: The mortgage company explains that the co-applicant's low credit score pushed the interest higher to protect the lender against a default; or, if the loan was denied completely, the spouse with good credit will likely request that the credit-reporting agency provide a copy of the credit reports used to deny the application. (That's a law, by the way. When denied credit, you are allowed to obtain a free copy of the credit report so that you can examine it for errors that might have lowered your score.)

Either way, the bad credit has surfaced. That could come as a shock to a spouse, leading to other marital tensions and questions of trust and openness that can taint the relationship for years. Better to disarm that potential by being up front at the outset, before the wedding vows echo. Painful as that might sound, consider this: Honest disclosure of your financial blemishes is far more likely to engender sympathy and a partner who's willing to work with you, as a team, to improve your bad credit. Hide the problem, and the moment it explodes into the relationship is the moment trust is destroyed. Such surprises are never welcomed.

If you're the one who learns of a partner's shoddy credit history, don't overreact. It's the result of past spending and repayment patterns that pre-date you. Yelling and screaming and getting bent out of shape will do precisely nothing to make the credit better. A smarter approach that serves to strengthen the relationship: Offer to work with your paramour to improve the addled credit. You can find all sorts of credit-improvement strategies online just by Googling "improve your credit." You don't necessarily need to pay for services that help repair credit; this is stuff you can do on your own, like paying your bills on time and reducing your credit card balances.

Even if you have outstanding credit, hiding debt or secret credit cards won't last long. Partners who heed the advice in these pages will wisely request a copy of your credit report to inspect for themselves as financial protection. They will ask to examine new reports on a routine basis as well to ward off financial catastrophe. Assuming your debt isn't held by a bookie down the block, whatever you owe will assuredly show up.

So, how do you ask such sensitive questions about assets and liabilities? Well, very sensitively. This is where emotion clashes with objectivity. Assets and liabilities are just static, unemotional numbers, a measuring stick of your finances today. Yet, people routinely seek to mask that measuring stick, largely out of fear of what the number implies. Does it imply I'm rich and, therefore, a target of feigned affections? Does it imply I'm poor and not worthy of your affections?

Does it imply I'm a penny-pincher or a spendthrift? With so much emotional baggage tied to the answer, asking questions like "So, how much do you have?" and "How much do you owe?" can be a mine-field.

One of the better ways into what can be a charged conversation is to offer your partner insights about yourself first, a strategy that tempers the anxiety because, simply put, you're going first. It's the elementary-school "I'll show you mine if you'll show me yours" approach to adult finances.

Start by announcing your goal: To pinpoint where you are financially as you embark on what you hope will be a long journey through life together, and that, as part of that, you want to establish a foundation for the financial intimacy—the communication—necessary for a happy relationship. Then, present a copy of your personal net worth, warts and all. This is an easy document to construct. Just list on the left side all your assets and their current value, then list on the right side all your debts and obligations. Subtract all your debts from all your assets and, there you have it, your net worth. With this, you are telling your partner, "This defines me financially; this is what you're committing yourself into, for better or worse."

Explain the good as well as the bad. How did each come about? Are you a consummate saver and enjoy managing your investments, and that's why your 401(k) plan is so healthy? Are you a consummate spender, and that's why your MasterCard debt sticks out like a crow in a bucket of milk? If you are burdened by debt, explain your plan—a legitimate plan—for paying it down or paying it off. If you save the bulk of your discretionary income, explain whether you expect that to continue or whether you see scaling some of that back to live your life with your partner.

After presenting your financial life, ask your partner to share as well, though don't expect the numbers to just come spewing forth. Most folks don't keep track of the totality of their financial life in their head. Likewise, don't be surprised if your request is rejected at first. Some people will still be leery of opening themselves up so completely for fear that you might judge them. Offer assurances that you won't—and then stick to your word, even if you're initially horrified that your sweetie is leasing that $120,000 Porche 911 Turbo, yet has less than $1,000 in a retirement account.

And, certainly, don't pressure your partner to act immediately; it could take a few days or several weeks to gather the data or muster the courage to feel comfortable being that intimate financially.

But do insist that this is information you must know about each other if the relationship is moving toward some form of permanency, particularly marriage. Remind your love that in combining your lives, both of you will necessarily be impacted by these assets and liabilities that you each bring to the party. As such, you both need to know what you are walking into.

QUESTION 6:
How Do You Use Debt?

Let's be clear: Debt is not evil. It's no different than a saw or a hammer—just a tool that, used properly, helps you build your future. But, as with a saw or hammer, debt used improperly can cause you and your relationship some serious hurting.

How two people view debt, then, will have a bearing on the relationship. Some people absolutely abhor debt, to the point that they're just short of wearing garlic around their neck to ward off would-be creditors. Others slather on the debt liberally, relying on creditors to fund a lifestyle their paycheck alone cannot afford. Mix those two personalities and you're waiting on an explosion if you do nothing to address the differences constructively.

Of course, most unions aren't so extreme in their approach to debt. Most couples fall somewhere in the middle of those bookends. Regardless, ultimately you both need to know about each other's views on debt, and what you need to know are the answers to these two questions:

1. How much debt do you each have?

2. What type of debt: credit cards, auto loans, mortgage, student loans?

The answer to that first question will obviously emerge when you're chatting about the assets and liabilities from Question 5. Still, focusing specifically on debt separately underscores its significance and the power it can exert over a relationship. After all, too much money has never driven anyone into bankruptcy, and couples don't routinely fight in the early years because they don't know what to do with the excess cash they've accumulated. You will, however, fight about debt because debt creates stress and anxiety, both of which create tension, which, in the context of a relationship, is the precursor to financial fisticuffs.

Here's the problem: Too many Americans treat debt like oxygen— they think they need it to survive. So, they whip out the credit card or tap into a home equity line of credit for every little want, regardless of its utility. That's bad debt, because if you don't have the means to pay for something with cash, then you don't have the means to buy it. Too many people, however, *do* buy it, particularly young people who have grown up in a culture where possessions are the tick marks on the scorecard of life or the means to happiness, however fleeting that happiness is. As such, by the time two people find each other and vow to live together, they've often mastered their MasterCard and they cross the threshold of a relationship with, not infrequently, tens of thousands of dollars in consumer debt.

Don't read that to imply that debt is best avoided entirely. That's a message many personal finance books push. And while certainly laudable, it's nevertheless unrealistic in an economy where relying on credit cards is easier and generally safer than cash. What's more, most people aren't likely to buy a car, and certainly not a house, with cash these days. Those costs are so disproportionate to most annual incomes that you'd save for many years, only to deplete your liquid net worth on, say, a house, then have to start all over again before you could afford a car. That doesn't really make much sense.

Obviously, those moments are better served by the use of a mortgage or auto loan, albeit one in which you invest some of your own money to buy an affordable house or car that fits comfortably within your budget. That speaks to an important fact to remember in your conversations about debt:

Not all debt is created equally, and not all debt is bad.

Running up $25,000 or $30,000 in credit card debt and auto leases? That's bad debt, and can be a sign of exceedingly poor money-management skills or an entitlement mentality that's quite likely to haunt the relationship.

Conversely, $25,000 or $30,000 in student loans or $100,000 in a mortgage is something entirely different. That's acceptable debt. That debt went to create the potential for a better standard of living through a higher-paying job, or the financial security that can accrue to homeowners.

Same with a mortgage: The debt should be affordable. A mortgage on a $500,000 dollar house when the family's combined income is $100,000 is bad debt because the monthly payment will consume an unhealthy amount of your after-tax income.

Some of the information you need to know about each other's debt personality will emerge while dating, so long as you pay attention. Little signs emerge in everyday moments, like always stopping on the way home to buy a $1 soda at the mini-mart with a credit card, even though there are cans of Diet Pepsi in the refrigerator at home, just a few miles away. Always eating out and charging the tab to American Express or MasterCard. Leasing or buying cars well beyond what you know to be someone's general pay level. A pile of bills on the counter that look untouched or that are in shambles. An unusually large number of credits cards in a wallet. Complaints about living paycheck to paycheck.

None of these are absolute indicators of how someone handles debt. Everyone does some of this stuff every now and then, and many do several of these things often—and none of it will ever raise a concern. Nevertheless, these can be signs of habitual problems revolving around the misuse of debt, and over time you will inevitably recognize that. Use these observations, then, as an entry point into the necessary conversations. Ask questions such as:

Do you generally carry a balance on your credit card?

A balance by itself is not immediately bad news. Many people carry relatively small balances that they can comfortably manage. They use debt as a tool to afford items, but they do so conservatively, never accumulating more than their ability to repay fairly quickly, as in two or three months at most.

The problem with carrying a balance is the cost, since credit card companies love tacking on that interest payment every month you carry a balance. So you keep paying added money every month to essentially finance discretionary, unremarkable purchases that you quickly forget, like a fast-food meal. Did you really need to finance a burger and fries?

Of course, the larger the balance, the larger the interest payment. Worse, many credit cards offer what are, at first blush, generally attractive interest rates. The company might offer a rate of 3.9%—maybe even 0.00%—to transfer your balance from a high-rate card, and you do, but then a few months later one of your payments arrives one day late because of, say, a federal holiday that shuttered the postal system for a day. The credit card company does not care about that. Your payment was technically late, and by the letter of the law—spelled out in legalistic gibberish in the contract agreement you assuredly did not read when you signed the application—the card company can jack up your rate to 29.9%, which it promptly does.

What you want to be wary of is a partner who is blasé about debt, who carries a relatively large balance, who generally only pays the minimum due each month, who continues to accumulate ever more purchases on the card, who's routinely buying new cars every couple years, and has various mortgages that allow for the purchase of pricier cars and homes. Those are glaring signs of someone living a life too large.

How big a balance?

Size matters—particularly when it's the size of your credit card balance in relation to income and liquid savings (liquid savings would be: cash, CDs, money market/savings accounts, mutual funds, brokerage accounts and the like, but not cars and houses or a collection of baseball cards). There's no single definition of "too much" debt. A load of $10,000 might be huge to someone earning $30,000 a year, since it represents more than four months of earnings that haven't yet been taxed. Then you throw in housing costs, utilities, food and transportation, and suddenly trying to pay off that balance is a struggle. But $10,000 for someone earning $150,000 a year is entirely different. That's less than one month's pre-tax pay—substantially more manageable, assuming this person isn't just paying the minimum due each month while continuing to amass ever more consumer purchases on the card.

A bad sign to beware of is someone who complains regularly about the bills that arrive, who receives numerous monthly statements from creditors or who has to split a purchase across two or more credit cards because the credit available on one card isn't enough. Remember: When you take a partner into your life, you're also taking your partner's debt. While you aren't responsible for paying it, you will still be subject to its influence on the relationship, whether that influence manifests as a partner's limited ability to contribute fully to the expenses or a partner's stresses and frustrations about always being in debt.

What's your plan for managing/paying off your debt?

You want to know that the person to whom you're committing yourself has some game plan for extinguishing the debt. "I don't know." "I haven't thought about that." "I'm going to win the lottery." "I'll just cash in part of my retirement account." "I'll ask my parents for the money." None of those answers is acceptable, and you should spend time understanding where those answers come from.

If you need to, work with your partner to draw up a plan to repay the debt. Some people who get engaged and are moving toward marriage even make debt reduction or elimination a stipulation of the engagement: The debt must be paid off, or reduced by a set amount— say, 75%—before you're willing to proceed to the "I do" section of this relationship. The rationale to use if you pursue this approach: "I do not want to start our marriage under a cloud of debt." When a partner questions that—and your partner probably will—be sympathetic, but defend your position with the fact that, statistically, debt is one of the leading sources of fights and struggle during the first five years of marriage. "Do away with the debt, and we do away with a big source of marital friction," you can say. "Plus, it means we have more of our monthly income to save for our new house, or to buy new furniture, to save for kids, whatever we want to do with it."

Did you pay for your car with cash, or through a loan or lease?

Paying with cash: That's good, the sign—usually—that you're dealing with someone who knows how to save to afford a big expense.

Who isn't using debt recklessly. Who is probably living within their means. Someone who's fine with delayed gratification. A car loan isn't so bad, either, so long as it's a loan for an affordable car—and "affordable" is obviously a relative term here, dependent upon a person's earnings, financial resources and other debt.

The potential worry arises when you hear: "It's a lease." A lease often allows drivers to slip into a car far more luxurious than they can otherwise afford. The reason leases are so popular is that they put high-end cars within reach of the hoi polloi. With a lease, you're not buying a car, you're paying rent on just that portion of a car you'll use— say, three years worth. In that time, the car will depreciate in value, from, let's say, $25,000 to $15,000. You're paying that $10,000 difference, plus interest. That's a lease in a nutshell. Such a structure allows folks to drive around in a sporty BMW for just $399 a month for five years (based on an actual example from mid–2007), whereas someone forced to rely on traditional financing would have to pay $670 a month for five years for the same ride. If you cannot afford $670 a month for the car, then you should not be driving that car, no matter how attractive the lease terms. Whether you want to accept this or not, the reality is that you're shopping out of your league, and you will never improve your financial condition doing that.

The message is this: Leases can be a sign of a financially indulgent personality, someone who pursues wants now because now is when the want strikes, damn the finances. That's not conducive to building wealth or financial security, and is certain to be a source of friction.

What type of mortgage did you choose when you bought your home?

Of course, this question assumes your partner owns a home. If so, knowing how that house was paid for is information necessary to your financial self-preservation. You do not want to go blindly into a situation where you'll be moving into your partner's home after agreeing to live together or after your wedding, only to find a few months or a few years later that a monthly mortgage payment that seemed affordable at $1,300 will soon surge to more than $2,000 and possibly move up from there to more than $4,000 a month. That might be just enough financial stress to send the relationship into an ugly tailspin.

We'll get into this more in Section Two, but just know that, like auto leases for a fancy car, certain mortgages, particularly interest-only mortgages and some very aggressive adjustable-rate mortgages (a so-called ARM) can be red flags that a homebuyer was unable to afford the house with a conventional mortgage and had to rely on a magical mortgage, instead.

To be fair, these mortgages can also indicate that someone is financially savvy, though possibly a bit of gambler because of the various risks inherent in these products. That's the rarer reading, though, and you will instinctively know when your partner has a strong background in personal finance. Most people are not "playing" the mortgage market as a way to bet on the direction of interest-rate movements, which is what pros do who employ these mortgages. Most homeowners are just looking for the cheapest, easiest way to get into the home of their dreams, and relying on magical mortgages is, for the most part, just another example of financial indulgence and shopping beyond your means.

Now, asking something like, "So, tell me about your debt . . ." isn't likely to engender much warmth or openness. To the contrary, the frank approach is more likely to erect a defensive wall, as your mate girds for an onslaught of highly personal questions and this unexpected financial interrogation.

A better approach is, again, to open your kimono first, so to speak. Offer up a copy of your credit report. I know—really, again, not very sexy. But money isn't always sexy. More often than not, it's prosaic and utilitarian. You can sex it up a bit inviting your partner on a date to a nice restaurant or even a weekend away, but announce your ultimate plan: "I want to spend a little time filling you in on my finances." Then, when the moment arrives to start the money talk, introduce the topic with something that speaks of togetherness like, "Honey, I'm really looking forward to us building a future together, and I want to show you my credit report and tell you a bit about how I manage my money, so that you know a little more about me financially, and you know what you're getting involved with." Be honest. Point out where your own blemishes lie. By making yourself vulnerable, and opening the conversation with hopeful expectations of your future as a couple—and by noting your own financial foibles—you disarm a situation that otherwise promises to be tense.

During this conversation, slip in a question such as, "Have you ever taken a look at your own credit report?" Your hope is that a partner will feel comfortable enough to willingly share either what they know about their credit report or even a copy of the report itself, though that's not guaranteed. Don't argue the point, don't fight about it, don't belabor it with all sorts of whiney "But I showed you mine . . ." Do, however, be prepared for the possibility that you will hear "no." Say something along the lines of, "OK, I understand. This stuff is sort of private. But if we're going to live together/get married we do need to talk about it at some point soon so that we can sit down and plan our financial future together. When you feel comfortable enough to share it with me, just let me know."

And if you are that person reluctant to open up, consider: If you're sharing bodily fluids—and all the risks involved with that—shouldn't you at least share your financial histories so that neither of you get burned later by something you never expected?

So, you're probably thinking: Um, where exactly do I find my credit report, anyway? You can download them online these days, for free, once a year, from each of the three major credit-reporting agencies TransUnion, Equifax, Experian—at www.annualcreditreport.com.

I'm a 760. You're a 520. Understanding Credit Scores

Few people interact with their credit score to any degree, so you might not realize that credit scores rule your life these days.

If you buy or lease a new car, take out a mortgage or home equity loan, sign up for a cell phone contract, seek out auto insurance or redecorate your home at a furniture store offering no payments until the next lunar eclipse, your credit score will come into play. Here are the basics you need to understand:

Credit scores, also called FICO scores, range from about 300 to 850. The higher your score the lower your interest rate. The lower the score, the more costly your life. Here's an example of what that means, taken directly from the website of Fair Issac Corp., which calculates credit scores. On a $216,000 mortgage, a credit score of between 760 and 850 means a lender would offer you an interest rate of roughly 5.9%, meaning a monthly payment of about $1,284. With a credit score in the 620 to 639 range, that same lender will offer a rate of roughly 7.5%, for a monthly payment of about $1,511. The end result is that you're paying an additional $227 a month—$2,724 a year—just because of your credit score. (These numbers, by the way, are as of press time; they change as interest rates change.)

What defines "good credit?"

Anything above 700 is considered excellent.

From 680 to 699 is pretty good, though your interest rates are somewhat higher.

From 620 to 679, you're in the OK range, but the rates you'll be offered mean your payments will be markedly higher.

From 580 to 619, you're in the low range. You'll still get a loan, but banks will be able to charge you much higher interest rates, and you'll probably be happy to take it because even if you don't know your credit score, you likely know inherently that you've got weak credit because of a history of missed payments.

From 500 to 580, you've officially hit the bad credit range. Not all banks will lend to you. If you need credit, you'll likely end up with a so-called sub-prime loan, a high-rate, high-expense loan that you will hate having. But you have no choice.

And below 500, well, there's not much to say. You're in serious need of repairing your credit. Now.

QUESTION 7: *Will We Operate from One Checkbook . . . or Three?*

This question really applies only if you're moving toward a wedding, because if you're living together outside the legal obligations inherent in marriage you really should not be commingling your assets or your money to any substantial degree except, maybe, in a joint checking account to be used for shared household expenses.

That said, couples who merge lives typically fall into one of two camps when it comes to merging their money: They either assume they must immediately join forces financially to prove they're united, or they insist that the only way to stay united is to keep their money separated. Neither assumption is necessarily wrong, though neither is particularly right, either. For instance: Launching a relationship— particularly a marriage—on a joint checking account just because you think you need to demonstrate unity isn't always the smartest send-off when neither of you has considered the shock inevitable when two people exert equal power over joint finances.

Then again, keeping your finances separate isn't always the best way to build intimacy and trust, nor is it a great way to build a financial future together. Such a wide gulf separates your money that, as a couple, you often have no idea the full strength of your combined financial might.

This idea of multiple accounts is a relatively new phenomenon, born largely of the fact that, statistically speaking, Americans are marrying at an older age, when men and women are established in their careers and their financial habits. Once they're thrown together and forced to manage money as a family, they struggle because they're each accustomed to their own ways of handling the checkbook and credit cards and ATMs—and those ways all too frequently clash.

Both approaches can work well, depending upon your situation. Before I detail the various options, let me say that there is no perfect solution. Each has its own strengths and weaknesses. Moreover, the choice you make now may not be the choice that works for you later. Personally, my wife and I have tried just about every approach imaginable, operating at various points from joint accounts and individual accounts and both types of accounts at the same time. They each worked for a specific period in our marriage. But about a decade into the relationship we ultimately settled on a single joint account because we came to see that shared finances made us talk about our money, made us think about what individual wants would mean to our family's situation overall, and both of those have ultimately made us better stewards of the money that comes into our life.

Ultimately what I'm saying is that as you go along in your own relationship, you will come to learn that managing money together is a process of maturity. Money is fluid. Same with marriage. You have to work at finding the rhythm that works as your experiences together change.

So let's examine the key ways that couples manage family finance:

Individual Accounts

In modern marriages, this is often the strategy of choice among new couples. Frequently, folks who decide to unite in a relationship have been on their own for so many years that they've grown accustomed to managing paychecks, 401(k) plans and credit cards their own way. And while you can certainly learn to rethink your approach to money, many people stubbornly refuse to, or they've come to learn that their financial personality grinds against their partner's.

As such, individual accounts can be a wise strategy if handled properly. If nothing else, they can reduce the opportunities for quarreling over the family's cash. After all, if you're each spending and saving your own money as you each see fit, and you've agreed not to challenge each other's financial choices, then no one has reason to gripe about where the money's going. Peace prevails.

In practical terms, individual accounts generally take shape as a "his, hers and ours" approach that allows for unified expenses like utilities and rent to come from that joint account (the "ours" account). Some couples run just a his-and-hers account that keeps all money entirely separate, with each paying some portion of those joint bills. Either way, the question is: How do you account fairly for the joint expenses? There are two basic approaches:

EQUAL SPLIT

This works well when earnings are vaguely similar. Partners essentially assign themselves selected bills to pay during the month, and then balance out at the end of each month who owes how much money to the other person. So, in a simplistic example, a husband agrees to pay the mortgage, electricity and insurance each month for a combined $2,500, while the wife agrees to pay the credit card bills for gas, food, clothing, entertainment and whatnot. If those credit card costs are roughly $2,500, then the couple is balanced and no one owes money to the other partner. If the credit card bills are less, the wife owes her husband half the difference. If it's more, the husband owes his wife half the difference. It looks like this on paper:

His Costs: $2,500

Her Costs: $2,000

Total Costs: $4,500

½ Total Costs: $2,250 (What each person should have paid for the month based on an equal split of the family's total costs.)

In this case, he spent $500 more than she did. To balance the scales, she owes him $250, or half the difference.

This approach does *not* work well when partners earn substantially different salaries. In this scenario, perversely, the one who earns the least is actually subsidizing the one who earns the most because the costs born by the lower-paid person consume a larger percentage of the paycheck, while the costs for the higher-paid person represent a much smaller financial burden. Such an arrangement is destined to fail.

PRO-RATA SPLIT

When salaries are obviously dissimilar, the pro-rata split is the better approach. In this setup, each person pays a sum each month relative to his or her income.

So, for instance, if you earn $100,000 a year, and your partner earns $40,000, then your salary represents about 71% of the family's combined income. Thus, you should pay for roughly 71% of the shared expenses, such as rent, utilities, taxes, phone, food, insurance and the like.

If you're both using the same credit card this doesn't mean you should pay 71% of the bill, however. Spend the time each month determining who's responsible for what expense on the credit card. Some expenses will obviously belong to one or the other person, though some, like, say, restaurant meals or those movie tickets, will be questionable. Maybe you split those in half, or along the pro-rata lines. Or the better approach: Operate with individual credit cards, as well. That way you each pay individually for what you each buy. And you can either split the cost of dinner and a movie, or one person treats the other.

There are a few things you need to remember with individual accounts. First, despite the promises you hear and read elsewhere, individual accounts *do not eliminate* money fights. In fact, they can create nasty little money jealousies. For instance, if your account is larger than your partner's and you can afford to buy those big-ticket items, your partner might pout about an inability to do the same and suddenly want the joint account to help pay his or her costs. You're mad your partner wants to raid joint money; your partner's mad because you seem so intransigent. That's not a hypothetical example, either; it happens all too frequently.

Second, individual accounts too easily create a financial veil in a relationship. And while you might be thinking, 'Um, yeah. That's the point," the truth is that these veils are ultimately bad news because you both end up operating in a shadowy world where neither of you has enough information to make informed financial decisions that impact the family as a whole. You don't have a complete view of your family's true financial picture. Small example: For years you've both wanted a new flat-screen TV, one of those really big, wall-sized jobs with high-definition. Problem, though: The "ours" account, from which flow all these shared expenses, never has enough heft to shoulder such a chunky purchase. So, you get by with a TV you don't want and lust after a TV you don't think you can afford. The reality: Tucked away in each of your individual accounts is plenty enough money to easily afford the TV. You just don't know this because neither of you knows how much lurks in the other's account. Moreover, from a mental standpoint people are often loathe to dig into "my" account to pay for joint wants, particularly if it means "my" account has to foot the biggest piece of the purchase to make it happen.

Walling off your finances is not a constructive way to build a life because it necessarily limits what you think you can afford to save or spend, which, in turn, leads to frustrations and feelings of financial inadequacy. In the worst case, these walled-off finances don't just mean you can't buy that new TV, they mean you feel financially insecure as a couple because the joint accounts never seems potent enough to afford you any breathing room.

Finally, the desire for individual accounts—and, conversely, the disdain for joint accounts—often is rooted in emotions, not financial logic. It's a push for autonomy and a way to evade the fear of, or prior experience with, powerlessness in a relationship. No one wants to find themselves in a situation where the person they're living with dictates what can and can't be spent, or reacts angrily, or even violently, to the expenses that show up in a joint checkbook register or on a joint credit card statement. To avoid even that possibility, people will stridently champion, or demand, individual accounts.

As a couple, you need to recognize this emotion exists, because it's not the easiest to identify in a discussion (argument) about whether you'll operate from joint or individual accounts. The sentiment, however, is often behind vague non-answers like "I don't know why I feel this way," or "Just because," or "It's hard to explain." If those rationales emerge, shift the conversation toward what concerns are bubbling up around loss of autonomy or a feared lack of independence, and what experiences nourished those feelings. This way you can begin seeking ways to work together to alleviate the concerns that exist and create stronger family finances. Maybe it's that you operate individually for a while and merge accounts slowly over time. Maybe you operate entirely individually but provide each other a monthly summary of account balances so that you each have a clearer picture of the family's overall financial health. The point is to talk and find that happy medium.

Joint Accounts

I was raised by my maternal grandparents, and every month my grandmother would sit at a desk in her bedroom paying bills out of a desk-register checkbook she shared with my grandfather. Likewise, my wife's parents have always operated from a joint account. That was normal operating procedure in their era, the way just about every couple managed the finances of living together under one roof. Part of the reason accounts were set up this way was that an older generation of women often did not work outside the home and, thus, had no income that necessitated separate accounts. But that doesn't explain it all. My grandmother worked for decades, well into her eighties; my wife's mother worked into her mid–sixties. Yet both managed to successfully live their lives financially within the boundaries of a joint account. They had the freedom to spend as they needed, they had complete access to the money, they had full knowledge of the family's financial wherewithal, they never had to seek permission to write a check or withdraw cash, they managed the account, they operated autonomously but also as team players.

That's what joint accounts are about: teamwork.

Despite perceptions, partners can operate just as freely inside joint accounts as they can in an individual account. More important, though, is the fact that responsible partners purposefully don't act so freely. By that I mean that when you funnel the family dollars through a single account that each person has access to you must, by necessity, practice a certain degree of restraint. Just as it's not fair for your partner to raid the account for selfish purchases, you can't go raid the account either. That might sound confining, and it is—from a purely self-centered viewpoint. From an inclusive viewpoint, this necessary restraint means you recognize that you and your partner must talk openly with one another about significant purchases. Maybe the family can afford it, so the purchase is pursued. Maybe the family can't afford it at the moment, so the purchase is delayed until the finances are stronger. Either way, what's happening here is that two people are communicating about what they can and cannot afford together, which, by turn, means you're becoming better stewards of your money, since you're not pursuing every passing fancy that you otherwise might if you were operating alone in an individual account.

Joint accounts limit the monthly hassle of balancing the check-book. With multiple accounts you have multiple opportunities to screw something up. Though a minor annoyance in principal, it can be a frustrating headache when it happens. Imagine it happening to two or more checkbooks in the same month. Joint accounts also lift any veil that might otherwise descend over the family's finances. When you both see exactly how much money you own and owe, to-gether you make financial judgments that are more informed.

The downside to joint accounts: None, if you handle it properly. Joint accounts works smoothly if neither of you exerts financial su-premacy over the account by, for example, asserting that because you earn the biggest paycheck you have greater say financially. That's a fallacy and it's condescending. In a relationship, you're both playing for the same team. Moreover, how are you going to feel when you lose a job and your spouse suddenly outearns you and starts calling the shots financially? And if you want some independence in a joint ar-rangement, well, allot each other a certain amount of money to spend each month without question—and then *don't* question it.

Personally, I've worked with joint and individual accounts in my own marriage, and my wife and I both agree the joint account cre-ates the greatest benefits for a family for one exceedingly important reason: Jointly managing the checkbook breeds financial honesty since no one can easily hide anything from the other. That, in turn, has helped us grow our wealth and work together to achieve our goals sooner in life than we ever imagined. To be sure, reaching that point took us the better part of a decade, so don't just dive into a joint ac-count if you're not yet comfortable with the idea. Wade into it with a his-hers-ours account that, over time, morphs into a single "our" ac-count. But whether you operate jointly or individually, there are three laws I've learned along the way that will help you succeed:

- **The Law of Autonomy:**

  This law holds that in a joint account, each spouse will be allowed to use a certain amount of money each month however they desire, no questions asked. That means you can spend it, save it, donate it to charity, bury it in a tin can in the backyard and your partner cannot utter a single syllable. This provides each partner a level of autonomy within the borders of the joint account, erasing worries that you'll get barked at for your financial choices. More to come on this notion of autonomy in Section Two.

- **The Sunshine Law:**

  This law holds that with individual accounts, each spouse will make his or her checkbook and other accounts readily available to the other, so that both partners have a complete understanding of the family's true financial picture. Moreover, this law requires that spouses agree to pool individual resources when doing so improves the family's finances or lifestyle. That means if the couple agrees to pursue a new TV or a vacation or an investment opportunity that the joint account can't cover alone, then you each contribute something from your own account to afford the purchase.

The law's title reflects a comment once made by former U.S. Supreme Court Justice Louis Brandeis that "sunlight is the best disinfectant." By opening your individual accounts to your partner, you are, in effect, shining light on your individual personal finances, helping instill a greater sense of financial security in the relationship—a key element in reducing the financial tension, stresses and discontent that can lead to money fights.

- **The Law of Equal Say:**
  This law holds that, regardless of the type of account you settle on, spouses each hold an equitable interest in every dollar earned. In turn, that means partners have an equitable interest in how the dollars are spent. Notice that last sentence did not say how "every" dollar is spent. That would imply a level of micromanaging that's certain to doom any family's financial plan or at least engender frustrations in the one who's feeling micromanaged.

Instead, make a pact in which you agree to discuss big purchases before they are made. Defining what constitutes "big" is up to you and your partner and your particular financial situation. Whatever the number, though, this rule applies across all family accounts, even individual accounts. Say you've lusted after a boat or car for years, and decide to pay for it out of your individual account. Sating that desire can ripple negatively through the family's finances. Even if you use money you saved, or maybe inherited, you have to stop and ask if the dollars would better serve the family by paying off debt, adding on to the house to account for a growing brood, funding a child's college account or investing in a retirement plan so that, as a couple, you two can live an easier life later. Ultimately, maybe you do spend your cash on whatever it is you want to buy. But that should happen only after you've both agreed on the purchase.

Women and Money

In part, the current trend of pursuing multiple accounts is a function of financial pundits who, in recent years, have been advising women in magazines and books that they must have their own accounts—their own checkbooks, their own savings accounts, their own credit cards—as a way to create their own financial identity and to protect themselves from husbands who might hide assets, are abusive, or run off with a secretary.

I understand the rationale, and in some instances that advice makes sense. Every women, for instance, should fund her own 401(k) plan or IRA if only because retirement will cost more than you imagine, and whether you remain married your entire life or end up divorced, a bunch of money in a retirement account is only going to help your situation. As well, every women should have a credit card in her name alone to create a credit history independent of her husband's. Establishing credit these days is as simple as proving you have a pulse. But the best rates and the greatest credit lines are generally for those who have long-standing credit in their name.

Beyond that, there are some real problems with this strategy that you should at least consider before insisting that all your assets reside in separate accounts. In short: Blindly hewing to this advice can do a disservice to women and relationships.

Foremost is the underlying message: Though not overtly stated, such advice is predicated on the idea that you will leave your husband or that he will leave you at some point. It can be perceived as a fatalistic, pessimistic exit strategy that creates unnecessary tension when entering marriage. If, over time, you begin to see worrying signs of impending doom in the relationship, then, in this case, you're justified in opening your own account and beginning to funnel some of your money into it with each payday to protect yourself and create a financial security blanket. But to enter marriage with the notion that you must immediately wall off your finances just in case the worst happens—or just to exert your independence—is the wrong approach.

In the 1990s, when the children of the Baby Boomers were just moving into the workforce, this strategy made some sense. This new generation of more independent women grew up watching moms financially subjugated by men who still hewed to tired but traditional assumptions that the Y chromosome imbued some privileged investment insight or a mandate to solely control the purse strings. Those women left the nest determined never to let any man dictate how or how much they spend or save. They refused to ever allow themselves to be dominated financially, to have to seek permission to buy something, or, the worst possibility, be given an allowance by their husband. Personal finance writers, picking up on this trend, ginned up this notion that women should take back their pocketbooks by building a wall around their money. A woman is to be the queen of her financial castle, with a moat to keep out the court jester.

I'm not saying that strategy can't or won't work. I'm saying that the people who advocate this approach fail to mention that you lose in the process something that's equally precious in a relationship. In return for your personal financial freedom, you forsake the financial honesty, openness and intimacy that work to strengthen a marriage.

You might fortify the "I," but you do so by weakening the "we."

The thing is, women can have it all—the financial independence that nourishes a sense of self-reliance, and the financial intimacy that nourishes a relationship—without resorting to a separatist strategy that seeks to partition her money from his. In large measure, that's ultimately this book's purpose—to help couples come together financially, not drive potentially destructive wedges between them. In a marriage of equals, neither sex should have reason to build a financial moat. For a woman, in particular, wide open finances provide greater clarity about all the assets and all the liabilities in the relationship. And as part of a couple that clarity gives you greater security and greater financial flexibility since the family's entire financial life is visible, rather than shrouded by individual assets and debts that are essentially hidden from the "we."

QUESTION 8: *How Should We Divide Financial Duties?*

Here are the possible scenarios for corralling the daily finances in a relationship:

- **One partner takes the reins of the family's pocketbook, and the other is all too glad to relinquish control.**

- **The partner assigned to manage the finances does so reluctantly, defaulted into the role because the other simply refuses to go anywhere near the bills or the checkbook.**

- **Both partners want to control the purse strings, but one claims the mantle through sheer force of will, leaving the other feeling usurped and unplugged from the family's money.**

- **Both partners share the duties, each taking responsibility for what they're strongest at or what they're most interested in or willing to manage.**

Given that you have no alternative but to pay your bills and deposit your paychecks at the very least, the above are the only viabilities that exist. A fifth option—neither person does anything—will work, but only for a brief period, usually a few months, before bills go unpaid, electricity and water are turned off, overdraft notices pile up, the credit card companies cancel your cards and call you daily, the foreclosure proceedings begin and your life is messier than a soap opera.

So this is where you must figure out how you two will manage the money that flows through the relationship once you're sharing a life together—everything from paying the bills and balancing the checkbook, to overseeing the investment accounts and buying whatever insurance coverage is necessary. Someone, obviously, has to handle this stuff. But here's the thing: All the duties don't necessarily have to fall to one person.

Two strategies you might consider:

GATEKEEPER

With this strategy, one person assumes all the financial duties, so long as the other spouse feels comfortable ceding control. The strength of this arrangement: the one serving as financial omniscient has clear view over the family's entire financial network, pulling the strings and pushing the levers in the right order so that the finances flow smoothly. It's a situation that can be very efficient when it comes to planning, investing, budgeting and shopping for financial services. The gatekeeper instinctively knows where everything is, how much money is available for whatever bills, purchases or investments the couple is considering, and how to move the various funds around to achieve particular needs.

But this model comes with two crucial caveats: The gatekeeper must make all financial registers, statements and transactions open to inspection, and the partner not overseeing the money must examine those documents to remain fully aware of what's taking shape financially, where the money is located and where it's going. Both of these are mandatory, and here's why:

For the gatekeeper:

In opening the family's books to inspection, you are including your partner in the finances and planning, helping to achieve a sense of trust and financial intimacy, and building a sense of financial security for both of you. That serves to alleviate any worries that can fester in your partner. Your obligation as the gatekeeper, then, is to provide a report monthly or quarterly—or on whatever schedule your partner requests—detailing the value of all family accounts, even individually titled accounts, as well as a list of where the accounts are located and the corresponding websites and passwords, assuming the accounts are accessible online. You must provide access to the annual tax returns (to prove you don't have secret income that otherwise must appear on a tax return, assuming you're not cheating the IRS as well) and a copy of your credit report whenever asked (to prove you don't have any hidden debt or secret credit cards).

For the partner not controlling the money:

In examining the registers, statements and transactions, you are taking the initiative to stay informed about your financial life. You never want to fall into a situation where you wake up one day only to realize that a gatekeeper has imprudently lost whatever wealth the family had, has rung up huge debts that you are now responsible for, has hidden a vast store of money beyond your reach or has put the family in financial jeopardy in some way. Your obligation is to peruse the reports the gatekeeper provides, and to file in a safe spot the latest report in the event you need to call on the information for whatever reason. Keeping track also means every year taking a look at your joint tax returns or your partner's individual return to ensure the adjusted gross income seems accurate (that helps uncover any hidden sources of income). Depending on the source, that income would generally appear somewhere in the "Income" section of Form 1040. Also, request to see your partner's latest annual credit report (that helps uncover any hidden debt, particularly credit cards you don't know about but for which you can be held liable).

The rule to remember: Family finance works best, and stress is reduced the most, when both partners know exactly what's going on with the money and where all the accounts are located.

TAG TEAM

With this strategy, you both assume some of the duties required to keep the family's financial life on task. Here, success means each of you takes stock of your individual strengths—your job skills, hobbies, interests, fascinations—and then structures the financial chores accordingly.

In practice it works something like this: If one of you excels at, or maybe just enjoys, picking investments, then anoint that person the family's chief investment officer, responsible for brokerage accounts, mutual funds, 401(k) plans, IRAs—basically, anything that requires selecting some asset to own. Likewise, if the other happens to enjoy, or at least can tolerate, a chore like, say, pulling apart the bureaucratic rigmarole that is the insurance industry, that person gains the title of chief procurement officer, responsible for obtaining the necessary insurance policies, filing the claims and fighting the battles when claims are denied or partially paid.

If one partner isn't well organized, that argues for the other to take control of the bills to avoid late fees and default notices. And if neither is particularly keen on the special torture that is balancing the checkbook each month, then switch off from time to time. Maybe you balance the checkbook one month, your partner the next. Maybe you trade off quarterly; maybe semi-annually. In fact, many couples often switch duties every so often, tired or bored by the same ol' same ol'. That's a good way to handle the chores in a situation where neither of you is particularly passionate about your assignment. This approach gives you a reprieve every once in a while.

The point is that with the tag-team approach, you're both getting your hands dirty, intimately involved with your part of the daily finances. You're helping each other handle duties that neither of you might want individually, and you instinctively have a more complete picture of the family's finances, which can't help but make you better stewards of your money.

Just like the gatekeeper model, tag-teaming requires that you communicate early and often with each other. After all, the chief investment officer has to know from the bill manager, for instance, that there's money available in the savings account or checkbook to invest in a mutual fund. Otherwise, just haphazardly drawing out the money risks an unexpected overdraft that costs the family unnecessarily and mucks up the finances for a while.

However you work the arrangement, find a division of labor that you're both comfortable with. And talk among yourselves—frequently.

QUESTION 9: *Do We Need a Prenuptial Agreement?*

Quite possibly there exists no two syllables more explosive to a relationship than "pre" and "nup." They instantly inject venom and anger into a conversation. Together, they represent one of the most hated legal documents in America, seen—rightly or wrongly—as a distinct lack of confidence in a relationship or a nasty insinuation that a spouse-to-be might just be a money grubber to defend against.

Of course, it doesn't have to be that bad.

Fact is, prenups aren't necessarily a raw deal for either partner. At their best, prenups can work to benefit not only the person requesting the agreement, but the person being asked to sign one—so long as you counter that your own prenuptial demands must be included in the contract. Recognize that all situations are different, and different laws apply in different states, so this isn't a legal treatise on how to structure a prenup or even an outline of who needs one. Such questions are better served by talking to a trusted adviser or lawyer. Instead, this is just to explain why a prenuptial agreement can be a useful marriage-planning document, and how to broach the topic without inciting your lover to riot.

Consider these simplistic examples: Your husband-to-be has a child from a previous relationship, and, prior to your arrival, he set up an investment account in his name but which is specifically earmarked for his child's future university education. Or maybe your soon-to-be wife has a disabled sibling unable to work or live unassisted. Her parents left her a $100,000 CD that, while it's in her name, is actually money for the disabled sibling should anything happen to your future wife. In both cases, both people have unassailable reasons for requesting a prenuptial agreement. Each needs to protect against the possibility that specific assets are lost in a potential divorce. Not doing so would be financially reckless for others in their charge.

Here's the thing, though: Your spouse-to-be approaches you over dinner and says, "We need to think about a prenup," and you're instantly on edge, because you don't know the rationale behind the request.

Part of the trouble here is that your future spouse chose the wrong way to introduce the topic. A better approach might have been to say something like, "You know my disabled sister? Well, my parents left me $100,000 that I have to manage for her so that she has money to provide for care if anything happens to me one day. It's not a big deal and this isn't a reflection on your or my feelings about you, but I have to protect that money for her, so can we talk about a prenup that would exist just to cover that money?" Yet not everyone chooses the right words at exactly the right time to explain their needs, so make sure to talk first about a prenup before instantly flying into a furor over the request.

So, how do you talk about a prenup without letting emotion spark a fight?

If you are the one seeking a prenup:

The best approach is be forthright about what you're trying to protect and why. Make it clear immediately that the request does not reflect your views of your partner's motives, nor does it mark a lack of faith in the relationship. In the face of a legitimate need to shelter assets earmarked for children or siblings, or to protect a family business or heirloom that parents or grandparents want handed down to the next generation, your partner will have a tough time denying the request. And if the person you've chosen to marry does argue against your request, or turns it into an referendum on the relationship, step back and reexamine your request . . . for marriage. You might have chosen the wrong the partner. Remember: Who you marry matters.

If you just can't bring yourself to ask this question, here's a trick: Hire a financial adviser that you and your spouse will rely on for planning advice in the future. Call ahead and talk to the planner about your prenup concerns, ask the adviser to raise the question for you, and it will be done. Advisers have no problem playing bad cop to your good cop, and they'll do it a way that sounds as though it's all part of the full-range of financial planning considerations for newlyweds.

When you're in the meeting and the advisor asks about the prenup, it might be that your partner answers with something like, "Oh, no, there's no need for a prenup," then looks at you and says, "right, honey?"

Answer with something like. "Right." Then pause, and say, "well, actually, is there any asset you want to protect? Because now that I think about it, I have a $50,000 certificate of deposit that has to go to my sister if anything happens to us. My dad gave me that money to manage specifically for her because he was worried about her lack of money-management skills, and I want to honor his request and protect this for her . . ." or whatever the story is that's germane to the asset you're trying to shield from a potential divorce settlement.

With this approach, you're announcing that you don't have a problem if your partner wants to protect certain assets from you, and you are providing a logical, acceptable reason for wanting to protect certain assets from your partner. More important, you're doing so in a way that clearly states your rationale has nothing to do with lack of faith in the relationship or concerns that your partner is just after you for the money.

If you are the person asked to sign a prenup:

Calmly listen to the need that's presented, then calculate for yourself: "Would I ask for a prenup if these roles were reversed?" If you can see the hypothetical need in your own life, then you'll likely not look upon a prenup as an indictment of your character or the relationship.

Of course, if the rationale for the prenup sounds sketchy, you have every reason to ask more questions to gain better clarity. You do not want to sign away your rights to make a claim on some asset in a divorce. Maybe you've never heard about these supposed children from a previous marriage and you rightly want to know more. And who wouldn't? If you're just discovering such relevant facts this deep into a relationship, you have to wonder about if other bones will fall out that closet and affect your life in the future. The same "who you marry matters" fits here as well.

Moreover, you might use this opportunity to protect yourself. Maybe you agree to the prenup, but with certain caveats written into the document that provide benefit to you in the future. Do not immediately shoot down a prenup request, but don't immediately agree to it, either. Express your understanding about the need, and tell your partner you'd like some time to mull it over. Use that time to talk to your lawyer about the document, to understand exactly what it is protecting, and how you might add language to protect yourself in the event divorce ever happens, noting, possibly, that in the event of divorce you will keep specific items that you know will come into the marriage, such as the family home or a second home you two are already talking about buying. That will erase one potentially large argument in the future.

Who needs a prenup? There's no ironclad rule that this person or that person does. It's a case-and-circumstances situation—as in, all cases have their own circumstances to consider. But, generally speaking, there are a few obvious examples where, regardless of whether you're a man or a woman, you should at least think about a prenuptial agreement:

- You own all or part of a business that you started, or that your family started, before your future spouse entered your life.

- You will receive a large family inheritance that you want to protect for the next generation.

- You own substantial assets accumulated prior to your future spouse's arrival into your life.

- You have financial obligations from a previous divorce or children to provide for from a prior relationship.

- Your future partner has substantial debts. (In this case you're protecting yourself not from the debt, since that cannot be tied to you to begin with, but from a lover marrying you to gain access to your money to repay the debt.)

- You have family obligations such as the need to care for elderly parents or disabled siblings.

- You own a family home that you and your family want to remain in the family.

Couples often think, "Why do we even need a prenup? Neither of us has anything to begin with."

That may be true, and maybe you don't need one. Or maybe you might and you just don't recognize that, yet. What happens if your spouse's career takes off and suddenly you become the trailing spouse? You're flitting all over the country—maybe various parts of the world—never building your own career, or tied to a single job or employer long enough to either qualify for or contribute substantially to a company-sponsored retirement plan. Then one day your spouse announces a love affair with a co-worker and wants a divorce. And to make matters worse, you don't live in a community-property state and, thus, you don't have automatic rights to half your soon-to-be-ex's retirement funds.

Beyond the heartbreak is the fact that you've spent your working life following and living your partner's dream, suppressing your own, and your retirement finances are anemic because of it. Sure, you might win some money in divorce litigation—then again maybe not.

A prenup could serve you well here, providing you with protection by requiring that your spouse fund a retirement account for you in the event the marriage dissolves.

So while you might be starting your marriage with nothing, you will certainly accumulate assets through the years that you don't want to lose in a divorce. Talking to a lawyer before the wedding about the ways a prenuptial agreement can protect each of you years down the road can save a lot of grief later. And if the marriage survives, you've lost nothing for your effort but a little bit of money . . . and wasn't love to suppose to win out anyway?

Though this seems a loveless suggestion, both of you need your own lawyer if you're going to pursue a prenup. One lawyer cannot serve both party's distinct interests. If you're asked to sign a prenup, have your own lawyer go over the document with you so that protections for you can be worked into the contract. If you're the one asking for a prenup, do not be surprised or offended if your partner requests time to first consult with an attorney. You're asking someone to bind themselves to a legal contract, and it would be financially rash for that person to do so without counsel.

QUESTION 10:
Who Buys the Rock?

Blame it on Pope Innocent III.

The thirteenth-century pontiff declared a longer waiting period for engagements, and, as a result, men sought a mechanism for bespeaking the fact that a particular woman was spoken for. A ring placed on the fourth finger of the left hand, through which runs the mythical *vena amoris*, the "vein of love," seemed a way to serve that purpose well. Early on, that ring was typically a small, simple metal band hewn from gold or iron. Then, in the late 1930s, a little-known South African mining company named De Beers repositioned diamonds, heretofore unrelated to marriage, as a symbol of everlasting love for the masses. A decade later, "A Diamond is Forever" emerged as an advertising catchphrase that would grow into one of the most successful marketing campaigns ever launched. Ever since, the diamond engagement ring has come to represent a source of consternation for couples pursuing matrimony. Who pays for the ring? Do we decide jointly how much to spend? How big must it be? Is small and flawless just as good as big and occluded? Whose money is this anyway? Does it make more sense to go with a less expensive diamond—maybe even a different stone—and use the savings for something else? If one of us buys the ring on credit, are we both responsible for paying it off?

As such, Question 10 is not as simple as it sounds. It's wrapped up in the more complex issue about how you two choose to spend money.

Going into marriage, the engagement ring is the biggest example of this question of how you choose to spend money, not only because of the cost but because so many tangential questions are entangled within it.

Assuming a man hasn't dashed off to buy a ring on the sly as a surprise, the engagement ring for many couples often marks the first major purchase pursued together. Therein lies a potential source of conflict, because while this conversation will naturally spin around the color of the diamond, the type of cut and the setting, the real issue is the cost of the stone in the context of other family needs. Too often, that "other family needs" notion is forgotten with this particular purchase because there are so many expectations and cultural conventions baked into the idea that a diamond somehow symbolizes love, despite how young that tradition is in the grand sweep of history. (For the record, I'm not playing stereotypes here and assuming it's the woman who's pressuring a man to buy a showy diamond. In many cases it's a man who's using an expensive rock as his mating plumage to show off or prove what a worthy provider he is. The reality is that many women don't want an oversized bauble on their finger because a) it's not their style, b) they feel uncomfortable or unsafe lugging around that much wealth on their left hand, or c) they'd rather see the money earmarked for other purposes that provide greater benefit to the family.)

It's not that buying an expensive diamond is good or bad. It's that the cost you incur necessarily has an impact on your finances, even if it's the man buying the ring with his own money before the marriage. That's money that otherwise would come into the marriage to afford other expenses for the family, like maybe part of the down payment on a house, condo or apartment; furnishings; the down payment on a new car; a respectable slice of an emergency savings account to create some financial security immediately; all or part of the honeymoon that you're putting on the credit card. Maybe it's enough to eradicate all or much of the debt both or one of you currently have—and based on that research I noted earlier from the Center for Marriage and Family at Creighton University pointing to debt as the leading cause of conflict early in a marriage, it's arguably a far smarter strategy to reduce or eliminate the family's debt than it is to use that money on a big diamond.

As such, there's a real conversation that needs to happen here that, while ostensibly centered on a diamond engagement ring, is actually about spending priorities going into the marriage. Despite the obvious emotions tied to the pending nuptials, this discussion should be purely financial. After all, if you've reached this point in your relationship, then it should be blatantly apparent that the love is there.

What you want to get to is this: What are our financial priorities as we start this marriage, and how do we achieve them?

Answering those questions means you must question all assumptions, including the assumption that the appropriate symbol of love and commitment should be a form of crystallized carbon equal to three months of the groom's salary, as the diamond industry wants you to believe. In a situation where this particular groom is earning, let's say, $50,000 a year, three months of salary (pre-tax) is $12,500. That is not an insignificant sum. Could you find a better use for that money?

How much sense does it make to impose such a high cost on a couple's finances just to symbolize love? And if you think about it, the true symbol of love and commitment is the simple gold wedding band placed on the finger during the ceremony, not the engagement ring. If you want to be truly thoughtful about symbols of love, then building a home together is a substantially greater symbol. So, too, is bringing a child into the world and having the ability to help that child build a better life through an education. So, too, is saving together for your future many, many years away. That ring on your finger will certainly mean a great deal, but looking back through a contented retirement at all you have accomplished in this life together will mean a great deal more.

Yes, exploring all the alternative, logical uses of your money is an unromantic, bean-counter way to consider an act as romantic as presenting a true love with a beautiful diamond. But there are the very real financial tradeoffs that exist.

Both people's lives are affected by the cost of an engagement ring, and both have a vested financial interest in how much is spent. As such, if you want to start your marriage as a good steward of money, then ask yourself if an expensive diamond truly benefits the family. Or is it just a flashy object for friends to coo over?

The Wedding Is Off! Who Keeps the Ring?

Many an engagement never makes it to wedding day. The show is cancelled before opening night for any number of reasons, and among the many questions that naturally surface is the one with, perhaps, the most difficult emotional baggage: Who keeps the jewelry?

In divorce, state law typically holds that the woman keeps the ring. Not so, though, when it comes to broken engagements. Courts in various parts of the country have ruled that the woman is obligated to return an engagement ring, arguing the ring is presented as a gift predicated on marriage. Break the contract—that is, call off the nuptials—and the ring must be returned to the donor, regardless of who backed out of the deal.

Not every state, however, has weighed in on this debate, and, thus, it falls upon the couple to figure out what to do with the ring. Depending upon the story behind the split, those discussions can devolve quickly into a nasty fight.

Based on broad cultural norms, here's what should happen to the ring when an engagement ends:

If the guy calls it quits, the girl keeps the ring.

If the girl calls it quits, she returns the ring.

**If the ring is a family heirloom, then the ring
stays within that family.**

As with so many things, though, exceptions to the rules abound. In situations where, say, the guy is caught cheating with or falls for another woman, it's hard to argue his fiancée should return the ring when she calls off the wedding. Likewise, if the woman's caught with her hand in the wrong cookie jar, well, there's little reason for her to keep the ring when her beau bolts.

Then there are a variety of complicating factors. What should happen, for instance, when a woman moves into her fiancé's house and helps pay his mortgage for a few years under the assumption this will be her house, too, one day, and then he nixes the nuptials? She has equity in a house that she has no claim to (go back and re-read the section on why commingling finances before marriage is a bad idea to begin with). If her man isn't willing to cough up some cash to compensate her, maybe she keeps the ring instead. Moreover, if a guy and gal shop for a ring together and the woman puts the cost on her credit card for whatever reason, and is paying it off, then there's a good argument for her to retain custody, even if she walks out on the wedding.

At the end of the day, every situation is unique, and while the ultimate aim of any separation should be to find an equitable split, in practice that doesn't always happen. Sometimes, you come up short. As Pat Benatar once sang, love is a battlefield. And not everyone leaves a battlefield as complete as they were when they arrived.

It's all just part of the adventure called love.

A Family Affair

Money Matters
After Marriage

Welcome to the rest of your financial life.

Now that you've exchanged vows, everything you do, or don't do, with money has direct implications on you and your family in a way that living together or spending and saving outside of marriage never can.

Until now, you really could act single, financially speaking, though you were sleeping in a double bed. Unless you opened a joint checking account or put both your names on the deed to a house, there were no legal obligations that bound you two together at the wallet. Now, there are many. Now, we're talking till death or divorce do you part—and either instance imposes financial implications that affect you, your spouse and your heirs in ways that simply living together never would.

So, starting now, personal finance is truly a family affair.

That said, let's begin with a sentence—a fact, actually—you should aim to remember:

Divorce destroys wealth; marriage creates wealth.

I don't write that just to dish up motivational pablum in some Pollyanna hope that you never seek a divorce. Excellent reasons exist for divorce, regardless of the financial impacts. In some cases, a divorce will do more to help you build wealth than would staying in a destructive marriage. Broadly speaking, however, divorce destroys wealth and marriage creates it. So says an Ohio State University researcher who tracked for 15 years the wealth and marital status of thousands of people. Those results, published in 2006 in the *Journal of Sociology*, found that folks who marry—and who *stay* married—accumulate nearly twice as much personal wealth as those who remain single or who divorce. Those who divorce are generally in the worst shape. They lose, on average, about three-fourths of their wealth, defined as net worth, or total assets minus total liabilities. That's a pretty good reason to work at your marriage when the inevitable gremlins pop up to test your relationship, regardless of whether those gremlins are financial or not.

Truth be told, while money is routinely demonized as the root of all evil, it's not the root cause of most divorces—despite that oft-quoted hokum about money being the leading cause of divorce in America. That supposed truism has been repeated so many times, in so many places and for so many years that it has become accepted wisdom. It's easy to see why, of course: Blaming a failed marriage on something as innocuous as money is socially acceptable and much easier to explain to friends and family than the real reasons that divorce happens. As such, you still read today in marriage magazines and reports from financial-service companies articles that toss out this commonly accepted data point.

Yet a researcher at California State University, Sacramento, found in a 2001 study that money is *not* a defining factor in divorce. He tracked married couples for years to find out what factors lead to the divorces that naturally occurred among his study group. In effect, he assessed couples throughout their marriage, rather than relying on them to self-report the results after the fact, when motivations are no longer as clear, the emotions have faded and it's simply expeditious to lay blame elsewhere. The leading reasons he found are the ones you might suspect if you stop and think about it: sexual problems, abuse, lack of emotional support and general incompatibility top the list.

Financial differences? Turns out money is basically useless as a reliable predictor of divorce. At best, financial woes accounted for about 5% of the reason any particular marriage failed, and more often it was about 1% of the problem, according to the research.

So, there's the good news: Just because you fight about money doesn't mean your marriage is doomed. It's not.

Instead, fighting about money is simply a sign that you and your spouse don't agree on some financial matter or that you both have passionate views about how some aspect of your finances is or, more likely, is not, working. Understanding what you need to be doing in your life financially, and learning to manage those fights is where you learn to survive financially as a couple, where you learn how to manage each other's financial expectations and where you begin to grow together financially. You can choose to find common ground and rarely, if ever, fret over some particular matter again. Or, you can suppress the fights because you "don't want to deal with this right now" and, instead, let the unresolved matters fester into much more explosive issues that you *will* be forced to deal with over and over again because you never spent the time working on a solution in the first place.

This second half of the book, then, aims to help you navigate the financial affairs you deal with as a married couple, when your daily life and your daily spending and saving habits become intimately intertwined. The purpose here is to help you build a stronger balance sheet for your family by improving the choices you each make about your day-to-day finances, and to help you find ways to more effectively communicate when differences inevitably arise.

Don't take the communication part lightly. That's where the breakdowns always occur and where the gulf is often so wide between husbands and wives. Five minus two is always three, and there's no way either of you can argue that fact in your checkbook register. But you certainly can argue about the fact that one of you doesn't do such a great job of remembering to subtract three from five in the checkbook, leaving the account overdrawn and subject to fees for bounced checks. The fight that this situation sparks won't come because there's some gray area in first-grade math. It will arise because there's a forest of gray space when it comes to how different people manage a checkbook—and so many other aspects of their financial life.

If you ever hope to gain control over money, you have to understand both the dollar-and-cents of money and the emotions of money. Don't feel like you're the only one who doesn't know this stuff. Few couples do. This isn't information that schools teach, and it's not information parents routinely dispense—often because they struggle with some of this as well. So you aren't expected to necessarily know this going into a new marriage. It's information, instead, that you piece together over the years through trial and error.

Combined, the raw dollars and the raw emotions are the two factors that determine the way money flows through your life. Learn how to manage both, and you're on your way to financial happiness, however you define that.

CHAPTER 2

MONEY AND EMOTIONS

Hold up a dollar bill—or a ten or twenty for that matter—and what do you see?

The answer you're not expecting is "yourself."

Money is a mirror reflecting who we are. That's fairly obvious on the outside. Look at all the people driving cars, living in houses and taking vacations they can't afford. They're using money to create a reflection of themselves that they want others to see. But money also reflects who we are inside: the fears, confidences, dreams and psychoses that define us. Someone who is inwardly paranoid about the future, about living in poverty or being subject to inferior healthcare when elderly, will tend to hoard money, often at the expense of living life. Though unhealthy, they can't help their actions because their brain is telling them that, at some level, their survival depends upon their ability to save now because the lean times are just a heartbeat away. They'll probably come across as a penny-pincher or a Scrooge to those around them, but those around them may not understand the depth of the worries.

Money is deeply powerful emotionally because it represents so much more than the ability to buy a Happy Meal on the way home from work. It is as much an emotional currency as it is a fundamental tool of commerce.

In the context of a relationship, it's rarely the money itself that causes a problem. It is the emotional baggage that comes prepackaged with the dollars that stirs up the trouble. That's where a couple's real money issues begin. You can't really understand where one another is coming from financially until you understand that there are emotions underlying the words you're hearing and the actions you're seeing. Begin to understand that, and you can begin to build a more robust financial life together.

To get to this point couples must master the toughest part of marriage: communication. The art of talking.

Life comes so fast that we, as couples, slip into a groove that can be tough to get out of. We learn to essentially grunt our answers at each other as we pass on the way out the door. We text message truncated questions and one-word replies during the day and feel like we're communicating: *Bills pd?* one asks. *Yup,* comes the reply. And that's the extent of the financial conversation for the week. That's simply not enough.

We don't sit and talk because that means missing out on the rest of our lives, the part of our jobs we bring home, the TV shows we want to watch, whatever. Talking just takes too much time.

I promise you, though, that if you get nothing else out of this book, your relationship and your finances will be well served if you learn to communicate with one another. Communication is at the core of everything the rest of this book is about. So that's where we're going to start this half of the book. But before we jump into the talking, we're going to start with an English lesson on personal pronouns.

Me + You = We

Marriage is not an individual sport. When you say "I do," you are joining a team, a fact that is hard for many people to accept early in marriage. They're accustomed to the single life and they still try to live that way after the wedding.

Joining forces financially is disconcerting to many a couple because the difference between "your" money and "our" money is so much more than a single missing letter. Everyone has their own ways of managing financial accounts and spending and saving the money they earn. When you're finally married and see these habits up close on a daily basis, you're slapped by the reality of each other's tendencies—or, as you're likely to perceive them, oddities. You can talk about these habits during your engagement—and you certainly should, as Section One made clear—but not until you're actually sharing the checkbook and credit cards everyday in a legally binding relationship do you fully begin to recognize, in some cases, just how fundamentally different you both are when it comes to money.

The question you must answer, then, is: How do we integrate each other's money style into a new family financial plan?

The first step: Recognize that you and your spouse are now a "we." You're no longer a "me."

That's easy to tell yourself, far harder to put into practice. You're accustomed to your own ways of thinking about money and handling the finances of your life, and by the time marriage arrives, you've been managing your money your way for a few years, maybe many years if you marry older. Change doesn't come naturally because you're not likely to perceive the need. If your way worked for you all these years, there's no logical reason you'd return from the honeymoon and suddenly think, "hmmm, I wonder if my way is the right way for the family? Better ask my spouse."

But here's the reality you have to accept: That independent you that once existed and once managed money in a particular way is but a memory. Certainly, you don't have to lose who you are just because you're married, but you do have to recognize that, by definition, who you are now includes another person. In fact, who you are includes another person by law in certain situations, since shared credit or joint ownership of assets imposes certain unified responsibilities and benefits.

Thus, marriage changes how spouses, personally, have to manage money. It's now a joint affair.

Consider this scenario, for instance:

Wife:

Confident in her ability to pick appropriate investments in her 401(k) plan and a brokerage account she opened after college. She saves 10% of her paycheck in investment accounts that she expects to grow into a formidable sum for retirement, and does a good job of picking mutual funds in her retirement plan and a few stocks in her brokerage account.

Husband:

Also saves 10% of his account. But has always been leery of the stock market, and is uncertain about all the options that are available. Since college he has allowed his money to accumulate in his checking account and, when the sum gets to a certain level, he moves the cash into a money-market savings account or a certificate of deposit.

In both cases, both husband and wife are doing the right thing—saving a meaningful chunk of their individual paychecks and investing the money for the future. And you can imagine that a basic, pre-marriage financial query such as "Are you saving for retirement?" would yield an answer acceptable to both: "Yes. I'm saving 10% of my paycheck." Everyone is happy.

Why, then, is this happiness fleeting?

Because the husband agreed to accept responsibility for paying the bills and directing the investments, and the couple never really discussed what that meant. So, the husband applies his financial norms because those norms have worked for him all these years, and the wife just assumes that the money the family is saving is generally being invested according to her definition of appropriate, her norms.

Only, the couple's norms don't mesh. When the wife discovers that cash sitting in a savings account and CD are her husband's version of appropriate, she's going to have a series of questions that could easily sound accusatory. He's going to respond with a series of answers that could easily sound defensive and that are based on his intolerance for the kind of risk she's comfortable with (and, of course, because this is how he has managed money his entire adult life). The conversation could become quite heated, and it's all because neither had a plan for integrating their individual personalities into their joint personal finances. Maybe such a problem never even crossed their minds—until it became a conflict.

Countless such scenarios exist. But no matter the situation, they all share a common trait: Lack of communication. Perhaps the real frustration you'll find is that this communication breakdown exists in part because you can't prepare for, nor even know every possibility that might arise. While you might have experienced some of your lover's financial quirks during the courtship, you won't know about one another's most annoying money traits until you're under the same roof for some time and forced to confront how you both get along with the finances.

So, you need to learn how to talk about money. It's a skill you'll need in every upcoming chapter, and, more important, it's a skill you and your spouse will need for the rest of your lives. Might as well learn it now.

Money Talks: Communication Without Conflagration

I've been with my wife for a long time, since the mid-1980s in one fashion or another. And for most of those years we never talked about money in any serious way. I would occasionally tell her about some investment I was making, or how well some investment had fared. Or, I would tell her about a raise I got, or question her on when her bonus check would arrive, or I would tell her our credit card bill for the month was too big and we needed to watch our spending. Rarely, though, did we ever talk in big-picture terms about our money, about what we both want from our money, or how well we were progressing toward goals that themselves were ill-defined in both of our minds.

We didn't really fight, per se, but we did raise our voices on occasion when she grew frustrated at me for being frustrated about some bill, or when I was frustrated at her about some expense.

It all came to a head one weekend morning at the kitchen table. I had just finished balancing our savings account register and announced the total, and she was entirely dissatisfied, leaving me nonplused.

Well, it turns out that she had been growing increasingly upset through the years that our savings account balance never really changed that much, always hanging around a certain level. She felt we were not progressing financially after all these years together.

The problem, however, was not our savings account balance. It was a complete lack of communication. She had no clue about the money that had been accumulating in retirement accounts, online savings accounts and brokerage accounts. I was at fault for not having communicated with her, and she was at fault for never having asked. We both had made wrong assumptions—me, that she didn't care; she, that I wouldn't explain it all to her—and, as such, had reached the tipping point where her frustrations boiled over.

A little communication all along the way would have prevented her not only from venting her anger at me, but from worrying the previous many years.

That's the thing about words: They say so much. And yet couples so often don't use them. Or, rather, they don't use them appropriately. When they do get around to talking about financial issues, it's often because of pent-up anger or some frustration in the moment. How much easier would it be to just talk all along the way to keep the destructive emotions at bay?

To steal a line from Nike, just do it.

All you need to begin talking about money—the good or the bad—is to simply open your mouth and say what you want to say. There is, of course, a right way and wrong way to do that. Opening your mouth the wrong way can cause a fight. Opening your mouth the right way can prevent a future fight. You obviously want to aim for the right way.

However, I'm not going to tell you what the right way is. Truth is, I have no clue, at least as it relates to your particular relationship. Every relationship is its own snowflake in that no two are alike. So whatever prescriptive advice I give you may be an utter failure in your marriage, and then you'll abandon this whole notion of communicating effectively and my advice will have been utterly useless.

Every couple communicates differently, and it's up to you to find the method that works in your life. My wife and I first tried talking face to face, but that led to tensions. We were so unfamiliar with that approach that we were naturally defensive when we felt our point of view was being attacked, and we were sometimes evasive for fear of being attacked—or for fear of revealing something that might put us in a bad light.

We found, however, that e-mail during the workday worked very well. We could say all we needed to say without interrupting or worrying that we were going to forget a salient point in the heat of discussion. We had time to edit our thoughts, which also gave us time to reflect on our own point of view and see the flaws. We had time to reflect on the other's point of view without feeling pressured to respond immediately or devise some on-the-fly solution. And, best of all, by the time we both returned home, the tension was gone because we'd had several hours to think about the matter, understand one another's perspective and come up with some ideas for how we might deal with the issue together.

E-mail gave us everything we had hoped for from a conversation.

I'm not saying that e-mail will necessarily work for you. It might. But, then again, maybe not, depending on your marriage. For some couples, a night at a restaurant is the answer, because talking about concerns and frustrations in a pubic environment keeps whatever anger might exist at a low simmer and under control. For others, a couple's retreat is the answer. Find a spot for a long weekend away from the daily chores of life and work and kids, and devote a morning or an afternoon to the necessary discussions. Or maybe it's a phone conversation that works best.

Whatever the solution, the point is the same: Use your words.

Don't blame, however. And don't use inflammatory words that belittle the other's feelings or actions. You want this to be productive communication. Blaming and belittling only elicit defensiveness, and you will ultimately go nowhere and generate a huge amount of fighting along the way. If you're mad that your spouse seems incapable of saving money, for instance, then address it by talking about your concern for the family's future, and how you'd like to revise your budget together to set aside a certain number of dollars every month in savings and investment accounts so that you can build a safety net for today and an ability in the future to afford all the things you both seek. With this approach you're not attacking your partner's spending, but reframing the dialogue. Suddenly, the conversation isn't about what your partner is doing wrong; it's about what you want to accomplish together, as a family.

As part of that discussion, you ultimately work together to fashion the revised budget (you *do* have a budget, right?). This new budget's aim will reflect that both of you need to watch your spending. To accomplish this, establish an amount of money you both can spend for the month. And to help seal the deal, allocate some of your money to your partner, playing it off by saying you don't have any significant purchases this month so you don't mind if your partner spends it. With this approach you rein in the excessive spending you despise, you have buy-in from your partner, and you avoid a fight by refraining from the blame and the accusations.

That's how easy it can be to communicate.

Of course, this assumes you have discretionary income in your budget to spend. If you don't, then you need to make it unquestionably clear that the family's current rates of spending exceed the combined income. Again, frame it terms of "family" so that you're not seemingly laying blame.

Such conversations will take some practice, no doubt. So don't be put off if your first attempts at talking to one another aren't perfect. Again, my wife and I struggled until we found a method that worked for us both. Once we had a feeling for how each other acts and reacts to money topics, we were increasingly comfortable talking face to face. But it took a long while to reach that point. In the meantime, we used whatever approach worked and we didn't give up.

Managing the Anger: How to Fight About Money

You are destined to fight about money. Anyone who tells they don't or haven't is lying. Couples fight about money all the time, though they might not define "fight" the way you or I do. Their voices might never escalate. But the differences of opinion surface in other ways, including silence, which is simply a passive form of a money fight.

So, fully expect that you will fight and that it's OK.

But along with "don't blame" and "don't use inflammatory words," you must control your anger when money fights arise. We humans naturally grow increasingly hot when we feel our message is being missed or misunderstood, and that's often the result in an argument. Passion does that.

Don't explode, it's the worst thing you can do. When you recognize there is a disconnect between how you and your spouse manage money, and you feel the anger mounting, stop and realize one fact:

Your partner may have no clue your frustrations even exist or that you're feeling flustered by some particular situation. Unleashing a torrent of unexpected vitriol isn't always productive, and risks sparking an unnecessary fight, because you are attacking your spouse for something he or she might have always done some particular way. And just because it's not your way doesn't mean it's the wrong way.

Instead of exploding, simply state your concern. Do not be sarcastic, don't taint your voice with a disapproving tone. Just be honest. You're upset/frustrated/concerned because you see X, Y and Z happening, and that worries you for these reasons. If you can't clearly explain those reasons, spend some time figuring out exactly why you're upset by the situation; if you can't explain your feelings to yourself, you're not going to convince your spouse that your concerns are legitimate—which will only lead to greater frustration for you.

Once you have explained yourself, don't expect a solution to be proffered or accepted immediately. Not everyone is capable of offering a well-reasoned answer on the spot to a weighty question, nor are they always ready to buy into your solution. Some people want time to cogitate on the possibilities and fashion something that makes sense to their way of thinking. That's OK, and you have to accept that. If you both can come to an agreement in ten minutes, great. Fight quickly, offer the solution, accept it, make up and move on.

If that's not the case, though, partners need to give each other the time necessary to think through the situation to find a workable solution. A few days, a week at most, is generally sufficient—though with large, life-changing issues like children, job relocation and other such weighty topics, a week may turn into a month or many months before an answer or solution emerges.

You can prepare for these moments before they ever materialize. All you need to do is acknowledge to one another that differences in how each of you manage and think about money will almost assuredly arise in your marriage, and that you'd both like to deal with these eventualities effectively and productively, rather than allow them to fester over time and escalate into problems that are far bigger than their significance. Agree that you will:

- **Approach one another when one or the both of you recognize that an issue is emerging or has already emerged;**

- **Give each other time to consider possible solutions;**

- **Work together to create and institute a plan that you can both live with.**

That's how you fight about money. You acknowledge that fights— or at the very least, disagreements—will happen. You address the issues when they arise and never allow them to reach the point that the anger explodes. And you refrain from the blame and inflammatory words that can turn a relatively minor affair into a hurtful episode that weakens your bond.

Financial success, as with any success—and marriage in general— demands work. Learning to communicate, and learning that me plus you equals we, are the two most important building blocks in that success. They alone are the foundation that will have you working together toward a unified future. And you will come to see that when you are on the same page as a couple, you are happier, more content, less prone to fights and more likely to reach the goals you set. What more could you ask for?

Does Money Equal Power?

In business, in politics and in Hollywood, the answer to that question is undeniably yes. Money fuels a certain swagger that translates into some version of power.

Marriages are funny that way, as well. He—or she—who makes the money generally assumes greater say in the family. Guaranteed, though, the husbands and wives who exert power because of their outsized paycheck are not going to concede that they use financial might as a tool of oppression, to control the family's pocketbook, or to slough off household chores they abhor.

Nevertheless they do, sometimes purposefully, sometimes unconsciously. Either way, the result has the put-upon partner feeling subjugated and less than equal in what is supposed to be a marriage of equals. Indeed, how husbands and wives exert monetary power can expose an inner dynamic that, over time, works to break down a relationship.

What might this look like in practice? Maybe something like this:

A wife earns a bigger paycheck and says during an argument about a new dress, "I make the money, so I can spend it how I want." Or, the husband earns the bigger paycheck and takes the position that he is already doing more than his fair share for the family, leaving his wife to deal with cleaning toilets and vacuuming the floors and taking the kids to school, the rule being that "until you earn what I earn, I'm not doing chores, too."

Those are overt examples, but financial power can just as easily be unspoken. The classic example: A husband works while a wife stays home with the kids. Even though she is clearly providing financial value to the marriage in the form of childcare, child transportation, and cleaning, shopping and cooking services, the husband exerts financial authority by deciding everything from the kind of car the family drives to the movies it sees to the investments it makes. In his view, he has earned the right to dictate the rules of the relationship because he earns the paycheck.

None of these are appropriate in a marriage. A relationship cannot survive—or, at least, cannot survive without resentments and anger—

when spouses are not on equal footing. The income earned in a marriage, even if you ultimately choose to operate from individual bank accounts, is "family income." It's not your income alone to do with as you want. Both spouses demand equal say.

Getting to that point of equality is the challenge. A spouse who is doing the subjugating likely doesn't realize it and may deny it if confronted. Or, they know exactly what they're doing because they're doing it for a reason. Meanwhile, a spouse who is being subjugated often doesn't know how to speak up or won't broach the topic for fear of causing a fight.

So, how to handle this?

In marriages where partners can talk about their concerns, they should move toward joint decision making. You both must have input into family matters, whether it's decisions concern where your kids will go to school, the new car you're buying, or the investments you're making. That means communicating your thoughts and designating a time to discuss the options you both find acceptable, and then establishing a middle ground. This works particularly well with big-ticket items, since these are generally infrequent, one-off purchases. It doesn't work so well, though, with the small, everyday purchases, where constantly discussing and negotiating matters such as what groceries to buy can be ineffective, time consuming and burdensome on a busy family. With those small items, divvy up areas of primary responsibility so that both partners have the power of the purse to make financial decisions for the family.

When it comes to movies, restaurants and vacations, if you can't decide together, then alternate. One person chooses the movie, food or holiday this time, the other picks next time. No fighting allowed. No fussing. No sour mood because you didn't get your way. Suck it up and get on with the fact that you're not living alone. If you want sole say over what you do and where you go in life and don't want anyone to question it, then you should not be married, simple as that.

And it goes without saying—though I'm going to say it because I know it needs to be said—that household chores are not gender specific. Toilets don't care who uses them, and they don't care who cleans them. A bigger paycheck does not provide a get-out-of-chores-free card. You can certainly operate like it does, so long as you're fine with the resentments that will accrue in your marriage.

The more problematic situations arise when a spouse purposefully uses money as a mechanism of control, or when a spouse is too timid or intimidated to vocalize the concerns. I'm not convinced that a person who maliciously subjugates the one they supposedly love harbors a desire to reverse course. If you recognize that you are married to such a person, this situation cries out for professional help from a marriage counselor with a specialty in financial affairs. (And if you are the one doing the subjugating, you're probably not likely to care what I say, so I'll just say good luck in keeping your assets in divorce court.)

For the timid spouse, this is going to sound harsh, but get over the fear and take control of your life. You must stand up for yourself. You must speak up for your financial needs and wants in your marriage, otherwise the bitterness you feel will consume you over time like a malignant tumor and you will begin to act out in unproductive ways, such as sneaking money from the family accounts through subterfuge, maybe getting cash back from grocery purchases for your personal wants, effectively laundering money so that a spouse doesn't see what's going on. You'll hide assets in secret accounts in the name of a friend, sibling or parent. It's easy to understand why you do this, but it's still ineffective over the long run. Better to confront the problem and begin to create a life you're happy with.

I can't tell you exactly what to do because there is no one-size-fits-all solution that will help every person and every marriage. I can tell you, though, that you must talk about this problem and work to rectify it so that you have a voice in your family's finances. This is just the sort of issue that will end in divorce. No one wants to feel like a second-class citizen in their marriage. No one wants to feel that they're powerless over their own life, or that they're being abused—and, in this case, the abuse isn't physical but financial and emotional. The marriage may last a while, but it won't last till death do you part. At some point, the spouse suffering the slings will vacate the marriage mentally and physically, and will seek a divorce or companionship in the arms of a more giving partner, which, in turn, will lead to divorce. Either way, such a marriage of unequals is likely doomed.

The best option if you're the timid spouse is to start with a counselor who can address your grievances specifically. And until you feel confident enough to discuss your concerns and frustrations with your spouse, you might want to meet with a counselor on the QT so that you don't stir anger.

Ultimately, both partners must reach a point when money does *not* equal power in a marriage. Allow that prevarication to take root in your relationship and you will struggle over the years with increasing levels of animosity and a reduced level of intimacy. And, potentially, a failed marriage.

Sex and Money

I know what you're thinking—and you're close.

Sex and money have been intimately intertwined throughout history and across cultures. But I'm not talking about the world's oldest profession. I'm talking about money and sex within a marriage—financial tensions can destroy a couple's sex life. If you've ever been caught in that special kind of hell, you know, in turn, that this leads to a new set of tensions, opening a new front in the battle of frustrations already raging in the house.

Maybe it's a situation where one spouse exerts dictatorial control over the finances or the other spouse is spending cavalierly. Maybe there's a trust issue at play when one partner lies about the finances and secretly—or overtly—spends the family toward or into bankruptcy. Maybe it's just that the stress of making ends meet leaves neither partner particularly randy. Whatever the cause, money is not only a powerful aphrodisiac, it's a powerful saltpeter as well, dousing amorous flames and, since a healthy sex life is essential to marital bliss, driving couples apart emotionally.

I was once interviewing a woman about the financial problems she and her husband were struggling with. He had overspent by $60,000 on home renovations without telling her, effectively wiping out their savings and racking up big bills on multiple credit cards; had changed jobs 8 times in 14 years, generally for no reason, leaving him with no job security, no consistent work history and no retirement savings plan to speak of; and had convinced her to cash in her 401(k) retirement account to access money. The ultimate result was that the family's house fell into foreclosure and the couple was forced to file for bankruptcy.

After detailing that litany of financial troubles, the woman I was interviewing said with a sigh of aggravation, "And he wonders why I don't want to be intimate with him. I don't trust him. If I don't shut down the sex, I will lose who I am, and I would be suppressing all this anger I have."

Their sex life, she said, had shriveled from multiple times a week to just once or twice a month, angering him and causing other fights. "The worst part," she said, "is that he doesn't think he's done anything wrong. He just doesn't see what the financial troubles he caused have done to me, to us."

Though there are certainly many reasons for sexual dysfunction that go far beyond money, if you find yourself wondering why your spouse seems uninterested in intimacy, or maybe you're the one who shuns it, make an honest assessment of your financial life. Do problems or stresses exist? Are you financially domineering over your spouse, or do you feel financially dominated? Is the debt level so heavy that the family's income struggles to meet the monthly repayment demands, creating an inability to save, build financial security or enjoy life? Is one of you using sex as a weapon to punish the other for financial matters you don't know how to address or may not even be conscious of?

Whatever the case, sex—specifically, the unexplained lack thereof—can be an indicator of financial turmoil that partners aren't always tuned into. People don't immediately equate sex with money in their marriage, but, as with the woman I was interviewing, money matters routinely bleed over into a couple's sex life.

Pay attention to the warning signs when you see them, or even think you see them, and you can begin to neutralize problems before they fester into something more difficult to manage. You have to assess this honestly. You can't tell yourself that you're doing no wrong and that the problem rests with your spouse. That will never get you anywhere and will actually weaken your relationship over time. Marriage is as tough an assignment as you'll ever have, and it requires you actually put some effort into the self-evaluation process. You likely know where the problems lie, you're just too afraid to address them or to admit that just maybe you're wrong. And, so, the manifestation is that your sex life suffers. It's the canary in the coalmine, so to speak. Sex dies when money is causing stress. Who wants to be intimate with someone they're increasingly mad at?

CHAPTER 3

HOUSEHOLD BUDGETS: OUR DAILY DOLLARS

Everyone generally knows how much money they have coming in every month; After all, you do see your paycheck when it arrives. Not everyone, though, knows how much money is flowing out. Therein lies the major challenge with budgeting: managing the expense portion of life. You might well recall the $1,200 you spent on a new mattress or the plane tickets to the Caribbean last month, yet few people pay precise attention to those little expenses, like the soft drinks you buy daily or the cheap lunch from the hole-in-the-wall down the block. But it's in those small details that successful budgets are built.

Knowing where you spend your money is the most powerful personal finance tool available, giving you the insight needed to stop spending stupidly on items that mean nothing to your personal happiness, while at the same time freeing you to spend on what's most important. It's particularly relevant information in a relationship, where two people, even if they do generally agree on big expenses, routinely have two sets of spending priorities that must be accommodated if both people are to remain financially contented. For that reason, there's a fundamental rule about budgeting and marriage:

Both partners must build the budget together.

Here's why: You must both speak up for your individual financial wants. All of us have specific expenses we want our family income to cover, be it a fatter savings account, more money going into investments, a new purse, a new suit, a country-club membership, whatever. We want to feel that our money is affording us whatever it is that makes us happy or secure. In effect, we all seek to be treated fairly within the context of our family's finances. That right there is one of the best ways to avoid money fights, because when your financial needs are met, well, there's not much reason to fight.

Don't read this rule to imply that every month you each must haggle over dollars like carpet merchants fighting over customers at a Turkish bazaar. The process should not be confrontational—and if it is, there are deeper issues at play, often stemming from one spouse trying to exert financial dominance over the relationship. This rule simply means that you both must be engaged in the process, as equals, so that you each know where the money is coming from, where it's going and how it's addressing your needs as a family and as an individual. If you despise this level of financial minutiae, that's fine, too, but you still must involve yourself to a minimal degree, if only to keep tabs on the flow of money through your life and to occasionally voice whatever financial wants and needs you might have.

And, really, budgeting isn't terribly difficult to begin with. It boils down to X, Y and Z:

- **You earn X dollars each month—your combined family income.**

- **You spend Y dollars in fixed costs each month—your mortgage/ rent, utilities, insurance, taxes, etc.**

- **You have Z dollars remaining.**

Those Z dollars are the crux of budgeting. They constitute your discretionary income, the money not already earmarked for the mandatory expenses of your life. Effectively manage those Z dollars—those discretionary dollars—and you are in control of your finances.

Making the Trade: Choosing How to Spend Your Money

On a macro level, how and where you spend those discretionary dollars impacts your ability to accumulate wealth. On a micro level, how and where you spend those discretionary dollars impacts your feelings of financial contentedness on a day-to-day basis. Think about that last statement by way of this simplistic example: You spend $6 a day buying a Slurpee as your morning, afternoon and drive-time treat, while your spouse is spending an equal amount on coffee. You probably never really think about the cost because in the grand scheme of your paycheck, these are affordable luxuries that have negligible impact on your bottom line.

At the same time, however, you both agree that building an emergency savings account equal to six months of fixed expenses is a wise goal, but you both lament never being able to find the money to properly fund the account. Well, here's a decent-sized slug of it every month—combined spending on workday beverages is $240.

You know the advice that's coming next. You read it in all the other financial self help books and personal finance magazines: If you'll just axe those daily Slurpees and lattes you'll save enough money to retire to your own island, or something like that.

But the advice you think you're going to read isn't the advice you're going to get. That traditional counsel—cut out wasteful expenses—is certainly the appropriate directive. But it's not always an effective directive. In fact, it marks the precise point at which budgeting goes wildly astray for couples. Because once you feel like your budget is a constraint that prevents you from enjoying life, well, then, there's really no reason keep that little tyrant around. So, out it goes. But that marks the exact moment you lose control of your spending, because you are no longer abiding by a budget. You're winging it. You might get lucky and stay within the confines of your income and actually save some money from time to time. More likely, you'll end up entirely uncertain of where your money is going and how much you're really spending. You will occasionally (or often) exceed your monthly income and you will have trouble finding money to save and invest. At the very least, it will be hard to buy something that's important to you without feeling like you have to go into debt or dip into your savings account to afford it.

The point of my Slurpee-and-latte example, then, is that you have choices. You just have to exercise those choices by deciding what is important to you and sticking by your decision. If saving enough to build an emergency savings account—or even to buy a new car—is a decision you make as a team, then you have the power to choose not to spend on Slurpees and lattes during the week so that you can achieve your goal.

If you find you can't live life without Slurpees and lattes, that's fine, and don't feel bad about making that decision. Again, successful budget management depends entirely on your ability to live within your budget and your feeling that your income allows you to enjoy the things in life you enjoy. Just go back and reassess your discretionary spending to find those items, or a combination of items, that will allow you to achieve your goal. Or, extend the period it takes to reach that goal. Maybe you cut out Slurpees and lattes every other day, or agree to buy only three a week. In doing so, you will have to postpone the date by which you expect to fully fund your goal, but so long as you're OK with that, then all is copasetic.

Ultimately, budgets are not about rigid rules. You don't have to forsake everything you like to build wealth and financial security. But you do have to forsake some things, because every choice comes with a trade-off. Money is an either/or/or game. You have $100: You can either 1) spend it on a new shirt; or 2) save it in the bank; or 3) buy a less expensive shirt and save the other part. That third option is what we're aiming for when it comes to effective budgeting: Make smart choices that allow you to pursue some of the expenses that make you happy, while at the same time save some of your money in order to build financial security.

With this strategy, you are in control of your budget, your budget is not in control of you. You're choosing how and where to allocate your scarce dollars rather than feeling crotchety about some budget dictating how you can't spend your money.

When you realize that you have the power of choice, you will feel better about your budget, you'll attain the goals you establish together, and you'll bicker less about money because your budget is meeting each of your needs.

A Penny Saved . . .

You read this everywhere, and you're going to read it again: You must pay yourself first.

You have bills today, I know. Those seem to take precedent. And they do— over your discretionary spending. But your savings takes precedent over your bills. Even if it's a relatively small amount you save, like, say, 2% or 3% of your gross monthly income, that money will mean a world of difference to you years from now when you're retired and living off the money you were able to save during your working career, and it can provide security and independence in the more immediate future if you lose your job or face some other financial trauma. In such a situation, having a reservoir of cash to dip into will mean you have an easier time weathering the crisis.

So as a couple you need to get into a pay-me-now mindset. That means consciously agreeing to save a certain amount of every paycheck and agreeing not to raid that account for consumer wants.

Here, we're not talking about savings that go into a dedicated retirement account like a 401(k) plan. You should most assuredly be saving in your 401(k) plan at work or, if you don't have access to one, then in an IRA (and we'll get to that in the next section), but dedicated retirement money is money that you cannot touch without paying usurious penalties before age 59½, so this isn't the kind of savings that will help you during a financial emergency.

I'm talking about a classic savings account, maybe a money-market account at your local bank, CDs from a credit union, or an online savings account. This is your life preserver. Indeed, before you start saving for a house, before you pay off all your credit cards, before you fully fund your 401(k) plan, you should start building an emergency savings account. If ever you find yourself in a bad spot financially, this is the account that helps you get to that light at the end of the tunnel, and it helps mitigate the financial tensions that lead to conflict in a marriage.

How much you need in this account depends on various factors, one of which seems to get short shrift in most financial media: emotions. How much money feels like enough to you? If you earn $50,000 a year and you're in the 25% tax bracket, you're bringing home about $3,125 a month. So if I tell you to save three months of take-home pay, or about $9,400 in this case, does that amount really make you feel like you have your life covered in an emergency? Personally, I keep a year's worth of my gross income—yes, *gross* income—in an emergency account, but that's just a function of my personal financial paranoia; in the event something ever happens to my job, I want to know from an emotional well-being standpoint that my family has the funds available to cover our costs for a substantial amount of time.

But that might not be right for you—or your spouse. You have to examine your finances from your own gut perspective. In general, though, you want somewhere between three months and a year's worth of income (net or gross, again you decide) in liquid savings such as CDs, money-market accounts or just a passbook savings account. Your goal is to squirrel away a nut big enough to pay for the necessities in your life if bad times strike. And "necessities" does not include dinner out and movies and the long-weekend trips to get away. Figure out what the absolute basics are that you must pay for every month: housing, food, utilities, transportation, children's education, insurance, property taxes, etc. These keep the family functioning day to day.

One of the best options is an online savings account because they generally offer the highest yields, and you might as well make your savings work as hard as possible for you. You can find a variety of online banks—such as INGDirect, EmigrantDirect and Zions Direct—by searching for them through Google or any other search engine. Because they operate in the virtual world, they don't have the same cost structures as brick-and-mortar banks and thus can afford to pay you sharply higher rates of return on checking, savings and certificates of deposit.

The easiest way to start and fund an emergency account is to make an initial deposit and then establish a recurring transfer that automatically deducts a prescribed amount of money from your checking account every month and dumps it into your savings account. Suddenly saving is effortless. Most of those street-corner branches typically require a minimum opening balance of $50 to $100. Many online savings accounts require a minimum initial deposit of just $1.

Fund this account regularly until you reach your predetermined level, even if it means you cannot pay off your credit card as quickly as expected, or you can't afford a new car as soon as you'd hoped. Emergencies never happen on your schedule, so you must be prepared for them at any time.

Four Easy Steps to Building Your Budget

One of the reasons people loathe budgets is that they often don't know how to build one beyond the obvious: listing your expenses and income, subtracting a few numbers and hoping they balance. Budgets are fairly easy documents, though, and are quick to build.

Start with the worksheet below (you might want to photocopy this, or, if you're computer savvy, build a spreadsheet similar to this that you can jigger with as needed). Don't be intimidated. This looks more threatening than it really is.

MONTHLY BUDGET

Month of: _____

HOME	Projected Month Total	Week # 1	2	3	4	Actual Month Total	Amount Over/ Under
Rent/Mortgage							
Property Taxes							
Home Insurance							
Telephone & Long Distance							
Cell Phone							
Oil/Gas							
Electric							
Water							
Household Supplies							
Furniture/ Decorating							
Landscaping							
Services (Pest/Clean)							
Home Improvement							
Maintenance/ Repair							
Total Home							

FOOD	Projected Month Total	Week # 1	2	3	4	Actual Month Total	Amount Over/ Under
Groceries							
Dinner Out							
Lunch (weekdays)							
Lunch (weekends)							
Total Food							

CLOTHING	Projected Month Total	Week # 1	2	3	4	Actual Month Total	Amount Over/ Under
Coats & Jackets							
Business							
Sportswear							
Lingerie							
Shoes/Purses							
Accessories							
Jewelry							
Dry Cleaning							
Alterations/Repairs							
Total Clothing							

SELF-CARE	Projected Month Total	Week # 1	2	3	4	Actual Month Total	Amount Over/ Under
Haircut/Hair Care							
Massage/Body Work							
Health Club/Yoga							
Manicure/Pedicure							
Facial/Skin Care							
Cosmetics							
Total Self-Care							

HEALTH CARE	Projected Month Total	Week # 1	2	3	4	Actual Month Total	Amount Over/ Under
Insurance							
Meds/Prescriptions							
Doctor							
Dentist							

MONTHLY BUDGET

Month of: _____

Glasses/Contacts							
Therapy							
Chiro/Acupuncture							
Vitamins/ Supplements							
Total Health Care							

	Projected Month Total	Week #				Actual Month Total	Amount Over/ Under
TRANSPORTATION		1	2	3	4		
Car Payment							
Insurance/ Registration							
Gas							
Maintenance (oil/lube)							
Repairs							
Car Wash							
Tolls							
Public Transport							
Total Transportation							

	Projected Month Total	Week #				Actual Month Total	Amount Over/ Under
ENTERTAINMENT		1	2	3	4		
Tapes/CDs							
Movies Out							
Cable/Satelite Service							
Movie Rental							

Theater/Concerts								
Sporting Events								
Magazines/ Newspapers								
Books/Hobbies								
Film/Photography								
Parties/Holidays								
Babysitting Costs								
Total Entertainment								

DEPENDENT CARE	Projected Month Total	Week #				Actual Month Total	Amount Over/ Under
		1	2	3	4		
Child Care							
Clothes							
Allowance							
Toys & Books							
Health Care							
Entertainment							
Sports/Camps							
Pet Food & Supplies							
Vet Bills							
Grooming							
Total Dependent Care							

VACATION/ TRAVEL	Projected Month Total	Week #				Actual Month Total	Amount Over/ Under
		1	2	3	4		
Airfare/ Transportation							

MONTHLY BUDGET

Month of: _____

Taxis/Buses/ Rail/Toll						
Lodging						
Meals						
Excursions						
Entertainment						
Souvenirs						
Total Vacation/ Travel						

GIFTS	Projected Month Total	Week # 1	2	3	4	Actual Month Total	Amount Over/ Under
Christmas/Hanukkah							
Birthdays/Showers							
Wedding/ Anniversary							
Cards							
Charitable							
Holiday gifts (Mothers Day, etc.)							
Total Gifts							

EDUCATION	Projected Month Total	Week # 1	2	3	4	Actual Month Total	Amount Over/ Under
Tuition							
Books/Supplies							
Fee							
School Lunch							

After-school care						
Fundraisers						
Total Education						

PERSONAL BUSINESS	Projected Month Total	Week # 1	2	3	4	Actual Month Total	Amount Over/ Under
Office Supplies							
Copies							
Postage							
Bank Fees							
Professional Services							
Internet Service Provider							
Total Personal Business							

INSURANCE	Projected Month Total	Week # 1	2	3	4	Actual Month Total	Amount Over/ Under
Disability/ Long-Term Care							
Life							
Total Insurance							

SAVINGS/ INVESTMENT	Projected Month Total	Week # 1	2	3	4	Actual Month Total	Amount Over/ Under
Periodic Savings							
Monthly Savings							

MONTHLY BUDGET

Month of: _____

Investments							
Total Savings/ Investment							

DEBT REPAYMENT	Projected Month Total	Week #				Actual Month Total	Amount Over/ Under
		1	2	3	4		
Total Debt Repayment							

MISC.	Projected Month Total	Week #				Actual Month Total	Amount Over/ Under
		1	2	3	4		
Total Misc.							
TOTAL EXPENSES							

INCOME	Projected Month Total	Week #				Actual Month Total	Amount Over/ Under
		1	2	3	4		
Earned Income							
Earned Income							
Earned Income							
Other Income							
Gifts							
Total Income							

		Beginning of Month	End of Month
1. Checkbook Balance	(+ or −)		
2. Cash on Hand	(+)		
3. Total Expected Income	(+)		
4. Total Money Available (1+2+3)	(=)		
5. Fixed Expenses	(−)		
6. Discretionary Income (4−5)	(=)		

STEP 1:

Pencil in all your known, fixed costs. These include:

- **Savings.**
  Go reread that sidebar a few pages back if you're not sure why you should include this in your list of fixed costs.

- **Housing.**
  For renters, this means rent and renter's insurance (and, yes, as a renter you really should have this coverage; it's not very expensive). For homeowners we're talking about mortgage, property taxes and insurance payments, which, for some homeowners, will be wrapped together into your monthly mortgage payment.

- **Utilities.**
  Electricity, gas, heating oil, sewage and water. In truth, many of these aren't "fixed" in the pure sense of the word, but treat them as a fixed expense anyway, since you must pay them every month to live. All will almost always vary from month to month, and while you could use an average, the problem is that half the months, out of mathematical necessity, will obviously be above average. So if you're expecting to spend $200 on electricity and in the oppressive heat of August your bill is $450, you risk blowing your budget that month and, then, fretting about it. A better approach is to use a number closer to your highest monthly bill. That way a big bill will never surprise your budget, and the smaller bills just mean you'll have money left over for several months—never a bad surprise.

- **Healthcare.**
  Monthly prescriptions and insurance premiums.

- **Transportation.**
  Monthly car note/lease payment, gasoline, insurance and annual registration, as well as commuting costs such as subway fares, tolls or train tickets, if applicable.

- **Education.**
  Student loans or tuition payments for yourself, a spouse or children. This might include before-school/after-school fees and a lunch program.

- **Life insurance or long-term-care insurance premiums.**

- **Credit card debt.**

- **Food costs.**
  This is groceries, not restaurants, which are discretionary. Grocery prices change and what you buy from one week to the next will often vary, so for the first few months just guesstimate this number until you see a spending pattern emerge; when you do, insert that as your fixed cost, but accept the fact that your actual grocery spending is likely to vary a bit from month to month.

- **Alimony/child support if you're divorced.**
  (This would obviously be a source of income if you were on the receiving end of these payments.)

For most families, those are the typical fixed costs, though you might have others in your particular circumstance. At the bottom, in the section labeled "Monthly Balance," tally these costs on Line 5, "Fixed Expenses." Don't worry about all the other lines at the moment; we'll get to them one by one.

STEP 2:

Figure out your expected income for the month. In most cases this is simply the after-tax sum of monthly paychecks, though other income could certainly make the list, such as alimony and child support, a bonus at work, freelance income, even the $25 birthday check your mom sends you every year. Add up the figures and insert the sum on Line 3, "Total Expected Income."

STEP 3:

Lines 1 and 2 represent the money you already have available to spend or save this month, money that's already in your checkbook or wallet. Money that's in your checkbook goes on Line 1. Money in your wallet, pencil in on Line 2. Add Lines 1, 2, and 3 together and write that sum on Line 4. This figure is the money you can spend for the month. Note: Line 2, "Cash on Hand" should *not* include money in your savings; that is not money you tap into for ordinary, monthly expenses. To do so would be to essentially undo all that you've done in previous months toward saving.

STEP 4:

All that remains is to subtract your fixed expenses (Line 5) from your total money available (Line 4). That leaves you with your discretionary income, the second most important figure in your budget (behind savings). This is the pot of money you have for all your remaining spending wants. Which means that this is where the hard part starts. Because suddenly family dynamics take over and the relatively logical process of assigning income to your expenses yields to the largely emotional process of who gets to spend how much on what they want. After all, there's not much arguing over the mortgage; it is what it is.

Life insurance costs what life insurance costs. Same goes for the water bill. But argue you will over how to spend the money that isn't already accounted for by your fixed costs.

To manage this process effectively, you have to answer together one question:

What's important to us this month?

Behind that answer might just be the biggest challenge newlyweds face. They want everything they want when they want it, eager to have their version of a perfect life immediately, and they're all too willing to whip out the credit card to obtain it now, never considering how they'll pay for the purchases later, just assuming the money will come from somewhere.

The Non-Emergency Emergency

This may be the best piece of advice I can offer you to help eradicate a meaningful slug of the financial stress that can ignite arguments between you and your spouse: Save every month for the routine, non-monthly expenses that pop up in surprise fashion every quarter or once a year.

I'm talking about the auto-insurance premiums that arrive every quarter, maybe annually. Quarterly and annual life-insurance premiums. The property tax payments that you don't include in your monthly mortgage statement. The annual educational costs for kids who attend a private or parochial school. The season tickets to a local sports team that you must pay for in a lump sum each year. Heck, even the big costs of an annual vacation that can seem daunting once you return and face the bill. All of this can cause stress when the bills show up in your mailbox because you're never expecting them at that moment, and your checkbook isn't equipped just then to handle that extra, unexpected burden. That can lead to arguments in the family because suddenly you're cranky and you end up taking it out on your spouse, who, in turn, gets mad at you for poor planning.

The Non-Emergency Emergency, continued

Yet this is so easily managed! Simply budget for these periodic payments each month and stick that money into a separate account that you only draw on to pay these bills.

It works like this:

- **Open a high-yield, online savings account that is tied directly to your local bank account. (Again, as long as you have it, make your money work hard for you.)**

- **Determine how much money you spend every year on all your periodic expenses—education, property taxes, insurance, vacations, whatever fits your world, and divide by 12 to get your monthly costs, even though you're not paying these costs monthly.**

- **Work that amount into your monthly budget, and every month transfer that sum into your online account from your local bank account.**

- **When the bills arrive, simply reverse flow—transfer money out of your online account and back into your local bank account, and pay the bill.**

I promise you: If you inherently know you have the money available to pay the bill when it arrives, you will feel absolutely no stress. You will not worry about where you're going to come up with all these dollars that you don't have in your checking account. You will not take your frustrations out on your spouse. You will not argue about or fret over the costs you can't afford at the moment. You will simply transfer a bit of money around, pay the bill and move on. It's a simple solution that will transform your financial life.

Tag-Team Budgeting

Every month offers up another batch of spending wants and needs: consumer purchases, fixed expenses you can't avoid, investments you want to make, savings you want to fund. You're ability to cover them all is likely pretty thin.

You no doubt can see the potential rub. Two people. One pot of cash. And the very real chance that your wants and needs do not necessarily match your partner's wants and needs. Whose spending takes precedent? In some relationships, this might never be a problem. In many relationships it will be, as each spouse offers input that the other disagrees with.

"We can't spend $500 on new clothes; I want to put
that money into our mutual funds," one says.

"I don't care about mutual funds," the other
retorts. "I work just as hard as you do and I want
to spend some of my money on new clothes."

Some version of that argument happens all the time between spouses, and it's not terribly conducive to creating that necessary sense of financial equality. More often than not one person imposes a decision the other doesn't like, or one spouse abandons the argument out of frustration, conceding victory for no other reason than fatigue. Either way, one of you ends up simmering quietly in anger, an emotion that will fester over time as this scenario plays out again and again—and again—as it assuredly will.

A better strategy is one you picked up in kindergarten: Learn to share.

Sounds simple. And it is. But that doesn't mean couples are always good at it when divvying up the month's income. To succeed, both partners must speak up for their own financial needs, and each must respect the other's wants as well. Doing neither risks building resentments over time that will erode the foundations of your marriage.

To get started moving in the right direction with tag-team budgeting, it can help in the early months for each of you to make separate lists of your spending needs for that month, putting at the top of the list your most pressing financial expenditure. Maybe that's a new suit for an upcoming job interview; maybe it's money for an investment. Remember, this is discretionary spending (and, yes, in this case money for an investment is discretionary. You should already be saving some portion of your paycheck automatically each month, so this is extra money that is otherwise allocated to whatever makes you happy).

Follow that with the second, third, fourth most important want or need, and so on. Then, sit down together as you're planning the budget for the coming month and fund your wants equally, up to the limit your income will allow, alternating between items on the list. In other words, your most important expense is funded, and then your partner's most pressing want. When you move down to the second item, your partner's is funded first, then yours. With item number three, it's back yours being funded first, then your partner's. Next month, you reverse the process so your partner's first item is the first one the budget covers. It looks like this in practice:

MONTH 1:	MONTH 2:
Wife's #1 expense	Husband's #1 expense
Husband's #1 expense	Wife's #1 expense
Husband's #2 expense	Wife's #2 expense
Wife's #2 expense	Husband's #2 expense
Wife's #3 expense	Husband's #3 expense
Husband's #3 expense	Wife's #3 expense

Don't expect to fund everything on your list. That's unrealistic for most families, since the vast bulk of us have limited resources to draw on every month. But that's OK, because presumably the items farther down the list aren't as important at the moment and can wait until another month.

With this approach, you're each spending some of the family's income on what makes you happiest, and you're doing so in a way that creates a level of equality so that you ultimately reach a point where you no longer need to make a list. At that point, you'll be in sync financially, routinely discussing income and outflow and making joint and individual spending decisions on the fly, neither of you feeling that you're being shortchanged in the relationship. I promise: That day will arrive, so long as you're both open and honest about your money, and you both accept that you each have equal say over all the money that comes into your relationship.

A couple of obvious concerns arise with this arrangement. One is price disparity. Maybe your top priority is a new pair of roller blades at $150, while your spouse wants a new business suit that costs $700. Such a situation is more likely than not. No worries, though, because you have several ways to deal with this. If your top priority is markedly pricier than your spouse's, then maybe your spouse gets to fund two or three priorities before you get to fund your second one. Maybe you two agree that if a priority cost more than some predetermined amount, then you set aside a portion of the cost over consecutive months before you buy it.

The other concern is self-imposed silence. In some couples, one spouse is intimidated by money, is intimidated by their spouse or is afraid to voice monetary needs for whatever reason. Often this is the case with women who come from families where Mom rarely spoke up about her financial needs and where Dad unilaterally managed the finances. In such a situation, it is incumbent upon the person managing the budget to ask, "Do you have any expenses we need to include in our spending this month?" This is also a situation where making a list of financial wants and needs for the month works well, since it helps the one who's intimidated make their voice heard, albeit in writing.

Different couples will fashion different approaches based on the different ways they interact. No matter, you just have to find the approach that works best amid the dynamics specific to your relationship. Don't be surprised if the first iteration you institute doesn't work. Money and marriage is a trial-and-error proposition, and all marriages—read that again, *all* marriages—suffer many trials and errors. So if your first approach fails, well, then, just try a different one and see how that fares over a few months.

It's Alive! The Living Budget

Though it resides on a piece of paper—or maybe on your computer screen—your budget is not a static document. You don't just fill in a bunch of numbers once and then go about your life. It is a living document that changes each month because your discretionary spending needs change. This month you might need a new wardrobe for a new job; next month you won't need that. Four months from now you'll need to fit into your spending the cost of a long weekend getaway to the Caribbean, but that's not an expense you'll have every month.

In short, life changes—and your budget must, too. For that reason, you have to interact with your budget every month, since every month you have the opportunity to determine how you want to spend the money not consumed by fixed costs.

In deciding how to spend your discretionary dollars, you have to be honest with each other. You can certainly agree to axe all restaurant outings this month and redirect those funds, instead, into some other expense. But halfway through the month, when you're jonesing for your favorite sushi bar or barbeque joint, you're probably going to rationalize a good reason to go. Do that just once and it becomes ever easier to do it a second and third and tenth time with other costs you've agreed to curtail. Basically, if you know that dinner away from home every Thursday night is important to the family, well, then cutting that out probably won't work. Your budget is keeping you from doing something that's not just affordable but that brings the family a certain amount of satisfaction and a sense that your income is providing for some of life's niceties. That's where too many couples slide off track: They cut the fun from their budget, slicing out everything except the must-pay expenses, initially happy with their pauperism on paper but ultimately disheartened when they can't live life outside their home because their budget won't allow it.

But don't blame the budget. Blame yourself for poor budgeting.

It goes back to being true to who you are and planning realistically. Yes, you have to cut discretionary spending to live within your means. Yes, you must set aside part of every paycheck to save and invest for the family's future. But, yes, as well, you must be a consumer to a certain degree, spending some of your monthly income for purchases that make you happy or keep you entertained.

Tracking Your Spending

How do you know you're on track financially each month? Or off track by a mile?

That tends to be the biggest problem with a budget: Few people can recall every dollar they spend during the day, much less across the course of a month. If you're not careful, you can easily rationalize extra costs that ultimately bust your budget.

What you need is a scorecard, a visual indicator of what you've already spent for the month.

You could spend a lot of time writing down the amount of every bill that arrives, but that's monotonous and you'll tire of that quickly. Besides, there are two easier ways. The only expenses you really care about each month are discretionary expenses—those are the ones that have the greatest potential to push you beyond your income limits. Those, then, are the only ones you need to focus on.

The first method is cash in the envelope. This seems simplistic, but sometimes the old, simple ways have survived for so long because they work.

If you determine that you can spend $500 a month on discretionary purchases (and, remember, this is after you've set aside money for savings), then you can spend the equivalent of $125 each week. Instead of keeping track of every receipt, stick $125 in an envelope that both of you can access during the week. When you need money, take what you need, and if you get back change from your purchase, put the change back in the envelope. If you run out of money before you run out of week, oh well; plan better next week.

This method forces you to pay attention to exactly how much money you've already spent because you can physically see your pile of weekly dollars shrinking.

Or there's the second method: the monthly spending scorecard. This scorecard, printed on the next page, will show you instantly what you've already spent during the month, and how much discretionary income remains before you run a negative balance. The beauty of this scorecard is that, on the fly, you can account for those extra expenses you didn't budget for at the beginning to the month. You just mark them off as they happen. In turn, that allows you to make adjustments to your remaining discretionary spending so that you don't overshoot your mark. So it might look like this: A college friend calls from the airport on a long layover and you spring for a $75 dinner. Earlier in the month you weren't anticipating this cost, but here it is. No worries, though; you just mark $75 off your scorecard and go about the rest of the month. You will automatically build that unexpected expense into your budget because as the check boxes fill up, you will slow your spending, curtailing other wants until next month, so that you don't exceed your limit.

Print a copy of this each month and check off the boxes as you spend. This is just a template; change it as befits your level of discretionary income. With this particular version, an "X" in each box represents $10 that has been spent. A "/"—or half an X—represents $5 spent. So, if you spend $25 at the gas station, then you mark off two boxes with an X and the third box has a /. Then when you spend $5 on lunch, you come back and fill in that third box with the other half of the X.

Round up or down. Spend $16 at lunch, and you mark off $15. Spend $18, mark off $20.

By tracking your money, you will never have to keep receipts longer than it takes you to get home, and you will always know exactly how much the family has spent for the month—an easy way to keep control of your budget.

MONTHLY SPENDING SCORECARD

10	20	30	40	50	60	70	80	90	100	$ 100
10	20	30	40	50	60	70	80	90	100	$ 200
10	20	30	40	50	60	70	80	90	100	$ 300
10	20	30	40	50	60	70	80	90	100	$ 400
10	20	30	40	50	60	70	80	90	100	$ 500
10	20	30	40	50	60	70	80	90	100	$ 600
10	20	30	40	50	60	70	80	90	100	$ 700
10	20	30	40	50	60	70	80	90	100	$ 800
10	20	30	40	50	60	70	80	90	100	$ 900
10	20	30	40	50	60	70	80	90	100	$ 1,000
10	20	30	40	50	60	70	80	90	100	$ 1,100
10	20	30	40	50	60	70	80	90	100	$ 1,200
10	20	30	40	50	60	70	80	90	100	$ 1,300
10	20	30	40	50	60	70	80	90	100	$ 1,400
10	20	30	40	50	60	70	80	90	100	$ 1,500
10	20	30	40	50	60	70	80	90	100	$ 1,600
10	20	30	40	50	60	70	80	90	100	$ 1,700
10	20	30	40	50	60	70	80	90	100	$ 1,800
10	20	30	40	50	60	70	80	90	100	$ 1,100
10	20	30	40	50	60	70	80	90	100	$ 1,200
10	20	30	40	50	60	70	80	90	100	$ 1,300
10	20	30	40	50	60	70	80	90	100	$ 1,400
10	20	30	40	50	60	70	80	90	100	$ 1,500

Division of Labor: Do What You Do Best

Perhaps nothing is as monotonous as managing life's day-to-day financial necessities. I'm not talking singularly about the obvious mandate to pay the bills and balance the checkbook. Daily life is filled with all manner of other financial matters that must be tended to: shopping for home, auto and life insurance; filing medical claims with insurers and then battling over reimbursements and deductibles; opening investment accounts and picking and overseeing the investments you make; organizing all the documents that need to be filed so that you can locate them when needed; collecting the information necessary for your annual tax returns and then either preparing the forms yourself or finding and dealing with a CPA or tax-preparation firm. This list goes on and on.

In many marriages, the division of labor generally happens by accident. Someone has to call the insurance company one day so, tag, that person is it next time any insurance matter arises. One of you does the tax work because you were accustomed to doing it in your single life, so you are suddenly the "tax expert" in the family. Or maybe one of you manages the investment accounts even though that's not really your forte, but you do it because your partner has no interest in it and, well, someone has to do something with these investment dollars. And sometimes who does what is purely a matter of control, with one or the other spouse laying claim to various tasks—over even the family's entire financial life—because they want the power to decide where the money goes.

None of these options are the best way to go through a marriage. No one should claim dictatorial control over the family's finances. No one should be burdened with every financial task that must be done. And no one should be charged with making significant family decisions about money without the other's input.

Instead, both of you need to figure out what you each do best, and then assume those duties.

Such a plan serves three purposes: 1) It reduces the load and the stress on the one person responsible for everything; 2) It keeps you both intimately tied to the family's finances, which means you personally aren't likely to be surprised by some unexpected financial disaster that can occur when only one spouse is running the money; and 3) It forces you to communicate with one another about various money matters since you have to talk about the insurance coverage the family needs, or the college-savings plan that makes the most sense, or transferring money from the savings account to an IRA, or whatever.

For tasks that neither of you want . . . well, someone has to do it. So flip a coin to see who gets what. Or, write each chore on a piece of paper, toss them all into a pillowcase and take turns drawing. The paper you pick is the task you manage. Every six months or year, switch chores, unless you've grown to like—or at least tolerate—the task you've adopted.

Don't fall into the trap that just because you're handling some particular task now, or you've always managed some task, that it's yours forever, whether you want it or not. I know a couple where the wife was a CPA with financial training, yet the husband managed the investment accounts—even though he hated doing so and felt uncomfortable selecting the mutual funds to own. That's ridiculous. Far smarter for them to delegate that chore to her since it's squarely within her professional orbit.

In my own marriage, this approach has worked to my family's great benefit financially. My wife is a registered nurse who understands the convoluted, arcane and downright asinine world that is medical insurance, billing procedures and reimbursement policies. Having dealt with insurers in my single days, I have about as much tolerance for the rigamarole insurers put you through as I do for pounding my hand with a hammer. Yet early in our marriage I was the one dealing with the insurance paperwork that arrived after doctor visits and such. One day, nearly a year after I'd paid a particular bill, our insurer sent us a check for $180, reimbursement for having paid the same $60 bill four times. I was ecstatic! An extra $180 for the month.

My wife; not so ecstatic, really. How could I be so careless that I would pay the same bill three times? I pleaded ignorance because I didn't understand who was billing whom, for how much, or even how much the original procedure cost. I just paid whatever bill came in. That was enough for my wife; she commandeered control of all things medical, and has saved us thousands of dollars through the years by spending countless hours on the phone reminding much-too-forgetful insurers that their policy does, indeed, cover some particular service or procedure that they wanted to deny; she has negotiated lower costs and had charges originally billed to us as part of our annual deductible removed and refunded back to us.

In turn, she has turned over to me all investment decisions, since she knows I have expertise in that area. Left to her devices, our entire portfolio would likely be stashed in a savings account and certificates of deposit. She has little tolerance for risk, understands only the basics about the stock and bond markets, and has only had exposure to a very limited base of banking products in her life.

That is the definition of division of labor. We both know we can count on the other to handle the financial chore that we individually despise, and to do so in the best interest of the family.

Recognize though that giving away a task can be laden with angst, so don't try to usurp power when you sense pushback. Sometimes managing a particular duty provides a partner a sense of security. In my case, it was the checkbook. I've managed my own finances since college, and I have a variety of reasons for wanting to know how money flows through my life and where the expenses are going, largely because I grew up with grandparents who struggled on a limited income. But one year I let my wife take over the checking account and bill paying when I was overburdened with work matters and had made a string of mental errors that resulted in an overdrawn check, a checkbook register that wouldn't balance and savings deposits that I'd forgotten to record.

But I was never comfortable with the arrangement. Even though I could easily look in the register to see what income was coming in and what expenses were going out and where our balance stood, I felt out of touch with my personal finances, and that left me agitated about our money. I explained that to my wife. She understood. And I reclaimed the reins to the checkbook—but with the proviso that I pay more attention to what I'm doing so that our bank accounts aren't so screwed up again.

Me, Myself and My Money:
Financial Autonomy in Marriage

From the moment you left Mom and Dad's nest, until the moment you paired off with a spouse, you lived an autonomous life, responsible to no one but yourself—and your creditors—able to spend freely on whatever desire, indulgence, necessity, need or want you had. Anyone could question your judgment, but no one could stop you from managing your money in whatever manner you wished. Spend like a drunken celebrity; pinch a penny like Scrooge.

"I do" undid all that.

Once you're married, you can't just decide, for instance, "Hey I got paid today; I think I'll spend my entire paycheck at the mall on the way home." As independent as you might like to think you are in your relationship, you're still spending family money, and there are consequences. That spooks many a newlywed, both young and not so young. Human nature strongly favors self-preservation. It's the reason people fear flying but not driving, even though statistically speaking your chances of dying in a car crash are 60 times greater than dying in a plane. It's all about the control. You're in control when you're driving, so that gives you a sense of security—albeit a false one. Buckled inside an aluminum tube, seemingly defying the common logic that gravity should not allow an 80-ton object to cruise along 40,000 feet above the ground, control is the last emotion you feel. Heck, you can't even see out the front window.

Financial autonomy slips easily into that framework. Money provides financial security, because it allows you to afford food, shelter, transportation and the ability to move freely; people are naturally fearful of relinquishing that security. They fear losing control over their life. That might seem overly dramatic until you're in that position and you have no access or limited access to your money. You can't make the decisions you want to make.

There are also demographics at play. We're a society that is marrying at an older age and, as such, men and women by the time they pair off have spent several years alone—sometimes many years—managing their spending and saving in whatever fashion they fancy, no one questioning those decisions.

Suddenly along comes marriage to raise questions. Spouses necessarily need to know about the family's finances for obvious reasons. Nevertheless, you can see the pending rift. When you're accustomed to a certain level of financial independence, and your partner expects a certain level of financial forthrightness, simple questions about where and why money was spent can sound like part of a police interrogation, and simple explanations can sound evasive. Queue the fight . . .

Marriage, by its very nature, erases a meaningful chunk of the autonomy you once knew. That's just the nature of the arrangement— and that's not so bad. Filling the void where your autonomy was is a level of intimacy that can be a far superior experience. To be sure, couples don't always see it that way. Freedom to choose how you use your money is a powerful emotion—as is fear of losing control of your money. In both instances you end up trying to tighten your grip over the dollars, but doing so generally intensifies the friction in your relationship, not unlike a rope being pulled inexorably from your hand. Clamp down tighter on the rope and what happens? The friction builds to such an intensity that the heat burns your palm. Let go before the friction builds and the potential for pain subsides. Either way, though, you lose control.

What you want is an acceptable equilibrium—a feeling of financial togetherness that's not confining, alongside a sense of autonomy that doesn't necessitate individual accounts.

There is a way of managing within a marriage this desire for autonomy. And you're probably quite familiar with it . . . an allowance.

Setting Up an Adult Allowance

Yes, I know; the last time anyone paid you an allowance, you were likely spending the outlay on bubble gum, baseball cards or cola-flavored lip gloss. I also recognize that to some people an allowance is going to sound paternal. Yet, the standard fare of youth can serve as a beneficial financial tool in marriage. Allowances allow both of you to spend or save in whatever manner makes you happiest, and you each have total control over your own decisions—which might be an allowance's most significant feature. In effect, allowances create a level of autonomy within the confines of marriage, yet allow the finances of the relationship to remain unified.

Making an allowance work, mechanically speaking, is straightforward. Together, you and your spouse agree to pay each other a certain amount of money each week or each month or with each paycheck, depending upon what the discretionary portion of your budget allows. And that's that. You each get to disburse that money however you want. The one overriding rule that cannot be breached: Neither spouse has any say over how the other uses their money. That means no snide commentary, no "well if I were you . . ." statements, no second-guessing, no rolling your eyes. In fact, you probably shouldn't even ask what your honey does with the money. As far as allowance money goes, you are a silent bystander.

There are a couple of ways to set the size of the allowance:

1. Establish a set dollar amount that you can each spend, such as $100 a week or $500 a month, or whatever fits your family's income level. You can distribute all of the allowance to each other on the first of the month, or you take it from the ATM at the beginning of every week, or you can take part of it out of each paycheck during the month.

2. Establish a certain percentage of the family's combined income that you can each spend, like, say, 10% or, again, whatever best fits your budget. If you use the percentage method, you must calibrate it based on combined family income so that each person gets the same allowance regardless of individual paycheck amounts. If, for instance, you earn $750 a week, and your partner earns $1,500, and you base the allowances on those numbers, you're soon to resent the fact that your spouse is nibbling on sushi for lunch while your allowance only affords fast-food meals. That arrangement isn't long for this world because of the animosity that will fester and ultimately erupt.

You don't need to physically pay each other this allowance in cash, although you certainly can if that makes the process work better in your marriage. But doing so could ultimately lead to a supposed need for individual accounts as the money you don't spend each week piles up and you want some place safe to stash it. Instead, pay the allowance virtually. If you're each allotted, say, $100 a week, then keep track of the receipts you collect during those seven days or check off your spending on some simple scorecard. It's not time consuming at all and after a week or two it becomes routine.

Now, if you do happen to operate from individual accounts and one of you happens to be a consummate saver and accumulates thousands of dollars, that doesn't mean you're free to spend it any way you want. Yes, technically you can. It's your money. But in practical terms you really should step back and ask how this large sum might improve the family and how spending it on what you want might affect the family. Is what you buy a one-time cost, or will it add an ongoing financial obligation to the budget? Buying a new car with your personal savings is nice for you, and might benefit your spouse to some degree, but an increased insurance payment necessarily impacts you both.

Likewise, would the money you've saved help the family pay to remodel a room, add onto the house or afford the down payment on a new home you've been talking about? Would it help pay for a dream vacation? I know it will seem unfair to some people: Here they've saved all this money for themselves and I'm telling you to go spend it all on the family instead. Well, yes and no. Some of it—maybe even a fairly large sum of it—should definitely go to your wants; you shouldn't be penalized just because you had the discipline to save.

But at the end of the day, being part of a family is an act in selflessness. And if the savings you amass can make life better for the family, well, then, that is money's highest and best use. Keeping with the idea that the whole is greater than the sum of its parts, family almost always trumps the individual.

One last rule: No matter how you set it up, you have to abide by the self-imposed spending cap. If you're just going to run to the ATM the minute you run out of cash, an allowance will fail you quickly.

Downscaling Your Life: Living on One Income, Not Two

In many a marriage there comes that moment when one of you starts thinking about quitting your career to stay home. This almost always coincides with the arrival of kids.

More often than not, this is a battle of the sexes, with women generally wanting to slip into that traditional role of stay-at-home mom, though here in the twenty-first century that's changing as more men pursue stay-at-home parenting while their wives conquer the business world. Either way, moving to one income from two often leads to a wellspring of torment and raised voices, since it means the family's financial situation will change. If a husband never expected his wife to seek such a life, and always assumed two incomes would be flowing in, the mere concept can be psychically bone jarring. This is months worth of arguments just waiting to happen.

But it doesn't have to work this way. Arguing, as I'm sure every couple with any experience recognizes, gets you nowhere. You rarely change each other's view and ultimately just agree to disagree, but not until after you've wasted minutes, hours, maybe even days carping at one another.

Instead of stirring up emotional discontent, tackle the issue together from a more logical, financial standpoint. Determine how best to achieve the goal, or whether the goal is even achievable at this moment. After all, a family is nothing more than a small business—you have income and expenses and assets—and businesses routinely jigger their operations to account for changing economic and industry situations. Families can and should do the same. In doing so, you might find you can afford the move, or you might discover that at this particular moment it's not attainable, but that you can get there in the next two or three or five years by restructuring your financial life.

So let's look at how you might go about building a new life on one income instead of two.

1. Tally Your Current Expenses

You need to know exactly where your money goes every month. This isn't a guesstimate. Guessing will only lead to trouble later when you realize that your guess was well off the mark and your life is more expensive than you imagined.

So, make a list with three columns—one for the expense category (mortgage, food, utilities, meals outside the home, etc.), one for the amount of money spent in each category, and the third to denote whether this is a fixed or variable expense. Track this back for three to six months, or track it going forward to several months so that you get a good feel for the range of expenses you pay in a given month, particularly those variable expenses that change from one month to the next.

Look over the list and whittle away at the expenses where you can. Variable expenses should be pretty easy to trim back substantially, and you're likely to find a lot of fat in there. If you have cable or satellite TV, for instance, can you switch providers to save money, or cut out premium channels that fatten your monthly bill? As for food, I promise you there is an artery-clogging amount of fat in your grocery bills.

Fixed costs can be thinned as well, though with more effort. Can you, for instance, refinance your mortgage and lock in a lower interest rate that will shrink your monthly payments? Losing half a percentage point on a 30-year, $250,000 mortgage saves $81 a month. That's not a ton of money, but it might be enough to make the calculus of a one-income family work. Similarly, look to re-price your insurance policies. Too often people find coverage for their car, house and life insurance, and never think about it again. Yet insurance factors are changing all the time, mortality tables are changing, new insurers come to town looking to build a book of business, existing insurers try to increase their share in a particular segment of the market. That means you can go shop your policies around, or combine all your policies with one carrier and reduce your annual premiums by several hundred dollars combined, savings that can also help make it easier for a family to live on just one income.

At this point, your goal is to cut from your expenses what you can, where you can.

2. Calculate Your Net Worth

You can't get to where you're going if you don't know where you are. Your net worth defines where you are. Figuring your net worth takes only a simple calculation:

a. Tabulate the cumulate value of all the assets you own—house, cars, stocks, cash, whatever. Base your house value on recent real estate sales in your neighborhood; check out car values at online sights such as kbb.com, the homepage for the Kelly Blue Book, the largest vehicle valuation company.

b. Tabulate the cumulate value of the debt you owe—mortgages, car loans, credit cards, home-equity loans and such. If you're unsure of the balance on your mortgage or car loans, call the lender and request a pay-off statement. They'll send you one in the mail.

c. Subtract the debt you owe from the assets you own, and the resulting number is your family's net worth. If the debt is bigger than the assets, you have a negative net worth, meaning you owe more than you own. If that's the case, going to a one-income family might not be the wisest pursuit right now. You both need to earn as much as you can to pay down your debts, otherwise trying to live off one income while repaying that debt could lead to financial and emotional stress.

The goal of calculating your net worth is to show you exactly where and what your assets and liabilities are so that you can think about potentially redeploying them to generate additional income for the family. It might be that you draw down your savings to pay off a credit card, freeing up the monthly payments that you would otherwise need to make. Or you move some CDs into real-estate investment trusts that generate above-average dividend income, increasing the money you have available to live on.

3. Tally Your Adjusted Income

How much do you and your spouse earn? How much money do you receive from assets that are invested, such as savings and investment accounts (do not include 401(k), IRA and other dedicated retirement accounts that you cannot access without penalty)? Do you own a rental property or another asset that generates income?

Add up all your monthly income, and subtract the salary earned by the partner who wants to stay home. This is your adjusted income, at least for the time being.

4. Crunch the Numbers

Subtract the current expenses you calculated above from your adjusted income. Is the result positive or negative? A positive number means you can live off one income.

In all likelihood, however, you're looking at a negative number—which explains why you and your spouse probably argued over this issue to begin with; one of you inherently knew that one income would not sufficiently afford your current life. But a negative number doesn't end the exercise, and it isn't proof that you can't live off a single salary. It's simply a mile marker on a longer road to where you want to be.

5. Re-Examine Your Financial Life

Now you need to go back through your expenses and really get down to cutting what doesn't need to be spent. Be realistic, and be creative. On the realistic side: If the two of you are accustomed to a date night once a week, don't axe it entirely; you'll only make yourselves miserable over time. Instead, trim it down to twice a month. On the creative side: If the family spends a week every summer at the beach, don't do away with that entirely; again, it will make you miserable and resentful that your one-income life can't afford what you enjoy most. Instead, look for a less expensive alternative, like renting a condo for a four-day stay instead of a five-star hotel for the entire week, or find a new vacation spot that's closer and less costly. Go through you entire list of expenses in similar fashion, cutting where you can, and rethinking ways to do what you enjoy in a less expensive manner.

Tackle the big items as well. Do you need two cars, or will one suffice if one partner stays at home? If you do need two cars, can you downsize one of them to a vehicle that consumes less gas and is less costly to insure? Can you downscale your house, reducing the size of your mortgage and, thus, your monthly payment? A smaller house should also shrink utility bills.

Examine the income side of the ledger as well. A stay-at-home spouse is certain to have some free time during the course of a day, either when infants are napping or school-aged children are in school. Those represent hours available for generating income in some fashion.

Depending on the stay-at-home spouse's career background, there might be opportunities to work as a consultant, possibly from home. Freelance opportunities exist in various fields, allowing for great flexibility in terms of managing a workload. You can also research the possibilities for starting an at-home business of some sort, given the wide variety of companies and products that operate on a home-based sales model. All you need do is Google something like "home-based business opportunities," and a world of possibilities pops up on your computer screen.

In some instances, you just won't find a way to get there from here— at least not right now. If so, the spouse aiming for the stay-at-home life must accept that the family can't make the situation work currently. But that doesn't mean the situation can never work. As such, both of you need to create a plan of attack for reaching the goal of living off one salary. One way to get there is to build a bigger savings account to supplement the single income. Follow those spending cuts you determined you could make, and bank that money for a year or two, or however long it takes to reach a level that allows you to supplement the one salary with periodic withdrawals from the bank account.

The point is that the one-income-or-two question is not one that you should either jump into lightly or dismiss out of hand as unworkable. Working together to trim expenses and find alternative ways of generating the necessary income can make a one-income life doable.

The key is that "working together" part. Arguing your individual points of view will get you nowhere, but will lead to increasing levels of frustration and consternation. Working together to map out the path that moves you toward your goal will ultimately strengthen the relationship.

And isn't a stronger relationship why you pursued marriage in the first place?

Gender Bending: Women as Breadwinners

We may be living in the twenty-first century, but in many ways money still flows along twentieth-century gender lines, particularly in terms of emotions.

Today, an estimated 30% to 40% of women earn as much as or more than the man in their life. And that can create unique tensions within a relationship. When traditional roles are upended it can cause conflict on the home front. And as today's gender roles become more fluid, expectations begin to shift as well.

Even if a husband and wife have jointly decided to operate as a one-income family, they may be surprised by their own unanticipated reactions. A woman can subconsciously lose respect for a man who earns less. Or, to elevate a husband's ego, she might demote herself within the family and fall back into a traditional role, making herself

responsible for primary child-rearing duties as well as all of the cleaning and cooking, despite her workload outside of the house. A woman
could also relinquish to her husband control of the family's finances
to artificially create the impression that the man is in charge of the
money. She may grow increasingly angry when she's been working all
day and comes home to a stay-at-home husband who is laughing and
playing with the kids. She may want to see herself in that nurturing
role and begrudge her husband for not earning a salary big enough to
allow her to stay home instead.

A man, meanwhile, can feel emasculated when he earns less, or
feel he's lost complete control of his financial identity in cases where
his wife is the sole breadwinner. He may feel that because her career
pays the greatest income, he should stay home with the kids. In other
instances he may try to overcompensate for what he perceives as his
own weakened state by claiming dominion over the finances, exerting
financial independence by spending family money freely, or by de-
meaning his wife's job or career while at the same time over-inflating
the importance of his own.

I interviewed a woman once whose experiences show how this can
play out. She was highly educated and worked in banking. Her husband
had two years of college but quit to work in construction. Her career
and salary progressed fairly quickly, while his progressed substantially
more slowly. Within seven years she was working in the lower executive ranks, earning more than double his income. Yet she felt obligated
to manage all the chores of home life, despite her travel schedule and
despite the fact that he spent many days at home because of weather
issues that kept construction sites closed. In private and in front of
friends and family, she told me, he routinely played down her career as
"cerebral and not very hard because she just thinks all day." His career,
meanwhile, required constant physical labor; his was "real work." He
pawned it off as a joke, and while she laughed in self-deprecating
fashion, she was steaming inside and annoyed by the belittling.

Nevertheless, she played his game. Though her banker skills argued to the contrary, she allowed him to control the checkbook, the savings and the investment accounts, unconsciously giving him a sense of power in the relationship. He used that power dictatorially, quashing her spending plans even while pursuing his own wants, including a new bass boat. She cooked and cleaned, often with little help from her husband, who regularly complained of being too tired after putting in such long hours on the jobsite, taking those opportunities to again downplay her job since it didn't include his version of manual labor.

He was certainly happy with the higher-standard of living that her income afforded the family, but continued to demean her "because," she ultimately realized, "he was trying to take my financial self-sufficiency away from me. He wanted to make me dependent on him when the reality was that his lifestyle was actually dependent upon me."

By the time she'd had enough, their relationship was in its dying throes and she hastened its ultimate demise by reclaiming control of her salary—opening her own checking account and having her paycheck directly deposited, a move that precipitated the expected fight. She filed for divorce not long after.

This is a mental game all around. If you think about this in simply the purest form, it's irrelevant who earns the most. Money is money and it doesn't care if it's earned by a man, woman or child. If a wife has the skill set necessary to earn big dollars, great; that leads to a higher standard of living that benefits the family overall.

Of course, we're into the emotions section of this book, and emotion is the biggest hindrance here. Both men and women struggle emotionally when the woman brings home the biggest paycheck. Logically, it should mean nothing. Emotionally . . . well, that's altogether different.

Here are some ways to deal with it:

1. Erase the Fairytale

Despite society's acceptance of the idea that the wife can be the chief breadwinner, many women still have, embedded deep in their psyche, the notion that a man is going to be the provider, a prince who will build them a castle. But it's flawed. If you, a woman, set out to build a real career, you're rewriting the script. That's not bad. It's just that in doing so you may one day find that you've progressed farther up the ladder than your husband, through no fault of his own. Be grateful for your success and the life you're able to help provide for your family. If you find yourself feeling resentful that his career doesn't match yours, stop and think about it for a moment. Different careers ebb and flow and peak along different cycles. Neither of you are in control of that, so don't hold it against him.

2. Disregard What Others Think . . . and Reconsider What *You* Think

Men are hardwired to believe that if they're not the provider, then they're a failure as a male. If you, the man, are feeling emasculated, re-examine your point of view. Consider your life if your wife quit her job and took one paying less than what you earn or are capable of earning. How will your lifestyle change? Will you have to move to a smaller house? Replace your car with something smaller or older? What will come of the vacations you can afford? Will you be able to save and invest for your future to the degree that you're able to now? Might you have to take your kids out of private school or stop saving for their college costs? What will you have to give up to afford the standard of living?

Easy for me to say, I know, but who cares who earns the most? I've been with my wife in some fashion since my freshman year in college in 1984. In that time I've earned more than her, equal to her and less then her. And at the end of the day it never mattered. I was happy that she was living up to her earnings capacity, able to help us afford a nicer home, nicer cars, better vacations and a fatter savings account than we would have otherwise had on my salary alone. I've always seen her paycheck as a benefit to my life, not a reason to begrudge her or feel less than a man.

While you're at it, recalibrate what it means to you personally to be successful. Is success only about the money, or are you happy in your ability to pursue a career you enjoy waking up to every morning, even if the salary isn't commensurate with your wife's? Do you enjoy the freedom of being at home with your children more than most fathers ever can? There are benefits you may not be focusing on because you're too consumed with the frustrations.

3. Appreciate Each Other

For men, appreciate the fact that your wife has the intelligence and the drive to succeed in her career at a high level, and that she enjoys her job. Her happiness should lead to your happiness. Appreciate, as well, the fact that she is helping you and the family live to a higher standard. You can't resent someone for striving for a better life and earning a bigger paycheck as a result.

For women, appreciate why your husband enjoys his work, even if it doesn't pay him as much as you make. You can't resent someone for earning less because just as your career is fulfilling, so, too, is his, and your life is better for it. The worst relationships are those in which partners are unhappy with their lives and their careers and they take out the frustration on those around them. If he's a stay-at-home dad, appreciate the fact that he's stepping out of the traditional male role to be a caregiver to your children, managing duties and chores and obligations that you would otherwise be on the hook for or have to pay for.

Elsewhere in this book I noted that men must recognize that a stay-at-home mom brings great value to a relationship in terms of all that she does during the day to keep the household functioning. The same holds true when the genders are reversed.

4. Share the Duties

Marriage isn't a competition. It's a union of equals. Ignore that and you might as well not be married because the relationship is doomed to fail. Neither husbands nor wives will tolerate for long a feeling of sharp inequality.

Equal partners share the tasks that must be done, both financial and domestic. A high-earner wife should not feel she must demote herself to raise the ego of her husband. Men are just as capable of cleaning toilets and taking the kids to school as are women. And a husband who earns less should not claim imminent domain over the family's pocketbook. Women have as much right to spend the money they earn as men have to spend theirs.

If you have to, create a schedule of duties so that you're both involved in every aspect of the family's upkeep. Pick a time to clean together on the weekends. Alternate cooking duties during the week so that you're either cooking together or are each responsible for certain nights. Manage your finances as a team so that you're both active in spending, saving and investing decisions.

5. Balance the Power

A lot of financial pundits will say the way to manage life when a wife earns more money is to operate from those dreaded individual bank accounts; that way you each maintain your own financial independence and, in particular, a husband won't be able to control his wife financially, and she won't feel compelled to cede control of her financial life.

I disagree. It's a perfect place, instead, to operate from a joint account, to which you both have an ATM card. As I've said several times, all the money coming into a relationship is equally owned no matter who earns it. A joint account with two ATM cards allows each of you equal, unfettered access to money, regardless of who pumps the most earnings into that account. It serves as an equalizer, because with separate accounts you risk the very real likelihood that the higher-paid wife ends up with a higher-octane bank balance that will, in turn, allow her to afford and do things her husband can't. You can smell the jealousy. (And for the record, the same holds true if the man earns the most.)

You still have to abide by the rules you establish for your family's financial life, meaning neither of you can raid the account for your personal wants, and purchases over a particular dollar amount must be approved jointly. But the higher-paid wife can't say or imply that because she makes the money, she decides how it's spent. Don't go off and buy a new sofa you love without your husband's input, even if he has no decorating sense. At least include him in the financial transaction. The same rule applies when genders are reversed.

6. Use Your Words

Sometimes, all it takes is a little communication to right wrongs, or perceived wrongs. Don't suppress your feelings, express them.

Surveys indicate that wives who earn all or the bulk of their family's income frequently worry about the consequences of losing their job. What will become of the mortgage payment and car note? Talk to your husband about those constant worries. Explain that you already feel like you have the weight of the family on your shoulders, for better or worse, and that you would like help around the house to relieve at least some of the stress you feel—not because you make more or he makes less, but because you're a couple and couples help one another to make life easier. Explain, as well, that you expect to have a hand in the family's finances and that you won't cede control or your ability to question unusual or selfish expenses.

As a man, explain to your wife why the situation leaves you questioning your masculinity, or why you worry that others might. If you feel embarrassed that friends or family tease you about the situation, or jokingly call you a "kept man," explain that to your wife. She's likely to be more understanding than you might imagine.

If you stay home fulltime with the kids, you might well feel you have no access to cash, no financial freedom and that others perceive you as a mooch unnaturally living off your wife's labor. That's a strong blow to the male psyche, and women excel at processing such emotional discontent. Tell her your frustrations, that you feel like you're seeking a handout every time you wish to buy something for yourself or even her.

Don't begrudge her that bigger salary, and don't throw it in her face every time you get into an argument. And remember this: Just because you earn less, you're not worth less. Your family just operates in a different fashion than others.

CHAPTER 4

HOUSEHOLD DEBTS: IN LOVE ... AND IN HOCK

If there's any money-management issue that's likely to cause consternation, frustration and fights—maybe even divorce—it's debt. Debt is invasive, pervasive and a potentially debilitating issue in a relationship. In love and in hock is no way to go through marriage, particularly the early years, because, statistically speaking, being in hock might just put the kibosh on the love. Debt, it turns out, is the leading cause of family strife during the first few years of marriage, according to research out of Creighton University's Center for Marriage and Family. That doesn't mean you're headed for divorce court because of debt, but it does mean that the accumulation of debt can undermine your marriage and cause dissention where none should thrive.

As such, while debt played a prominent role in the questions to ask a future spouse in Section One, the role it promises to play once you're married is so much bigger that we have to address it again here.

But go into these next several pages knowing that debt is not an evil word. Nor is debt inherently bad. Good debt exists, including a mortgage on an affordable home, and we'll get to that in a short bit.

Before you do anything to address the idea of debt, though, you need to determine how you two expect to employ debt in your life. Are you going to use your credit card to support your lifestyle beyond what your paychecks can handle? Will you carry a credit card balance for a few years and pay it off as your income increases or as you earn bonuses? Will you pay off your balance monthly and limit your credit card use to only what you can afford that month? You might know your answer to those questions, but do you know your spouse's answer?

What we're going to start with, then, is developing a debt philosophy.

Formulating a Debt Philosophy

If you're familiar with the movie *Jerry Maguire*, you're undoubtedly familiar with the line "It was *just* a mission statement!" Well, a debt philosophy is no more difficult than formulating the financial mission statement you will adhere to as a family.

Your debt philosophy serves as the structural foundation of your family's beliefs when it comes to the dos and don'ts of debt. This doesn't need to be some deep, profound statement. It can be something simple and succinct. Something like:

> We agree together to purposefully live below our means, not to pursue material wants without the money to afford them, never to use emergency savings for consumer purchases, and to take on debt only when it benefits the family's long-term goals or needs.

That's all you need. Now, don't adopt the one above and call it done. Your family has its own specific needs to address, and no doubt you each have your own beliefs about debt. So fashion a philosophy together that jibes with how you both feel. In coming up with your debt philosophy, you'll want to determine answers to questions such as:

- **Will we pay cash for everyday purchases like groceries and gas or accumulate those costs on a credit card?**

- Will we pay off our credit card every month, or are we comfortable carrying a balance—and, if so, how big a balance?

- Will we refrain from spending more than our monthly income, or can we occasionally overspend to afford a purchase like a new sofa or a vacation? And if we do buy large purchases on credit, how soon will we pay them off?

- Will our savings account remain untouchable except for emergencies, or can we occasionally dip into it to afford certain expenses?

- What defines an emergency expense?

Couples on the same page philosophically should have little trouble designing a debt philosophy appropriate to their lives. The likeliest breakdowns will occur with couples who have sharply divergent views of debt. For those couples, success will come through compromise. For instance: Will savings remain untouchable except for emergencies? One might answer "absolutely," while the other says, "no way." Split the middle in some fashion by, possibly, creating an agreed-upon level below which the savings account will not be allowed to fall outside of a true emergency. Or agree to an amount that can be occasionally spent for items that benefit the family broadly. But you must define "occasionally" and what those beneficial expenses are. Maybe it's that once a year the savings account is allowed to kick in $1,000 to help cover the costs of a vacation that the family's monthly finances can't entirely cover alone—so long as taking that money doesn't drop the savings below some agreed-upon minimum level.

And then, stick to your debt philosophy. Don't massage it just because it doesn't fit your needs at the moment. Remember, you designed this philosophy in a sober moment. Don't renege on it when you're drunk on the thought of affording some nifty something or other that you really want.

How Will You Use Debt?

Let's back up a step and look at why couples even need to create a debt philosophy.

Spouses today routinely enter marriage already laden with various forms of debt. There are student loans and car loans and leases, and maybe store-branded charge cards used to buy clothes or to furnish an apartment or condo. And certainly there's the credit card debt for all sort of discretionary purchases that one or the both of you have racked up. Whatever the case, all this debt is akin to showing up on your wedding day with a negative dowry. No matter whether you decide to combine finances or maintain separate accounts, this pre-marital debt necessarily becomes a wart that affects you both, since the mandatory debt payments that you make jointly or individually will undeniably reduce the amount of money the family has for other purposes.

That alone argues for partners to spend much time talking about debt before and, particularly, after marriage.

How—and this is exactly the kind of question your debt philosophy should answer—will you use debt? To buy necessities and discretionary purchases that, based on your budget, you'll pay off every month so that you don't accumulate interest on a credit card balance? Or to buy costlier items your income can't afford, so you'll carry a credit card balance and pay interest charges that reduce your ability to save?

How will you pay off the debt amassed prior to marriage? Is that the sole responsibility of the person lugging the debt into the relationship? Or will you work together to pay it off from the family's joint income?

Where do debt and savings rank among your list of priorities? Do you want to pay off all your debt before you begin to build a savings cushion? (I'd argue that's not a great idea; you never know when a financial emergency will rise up.) Or do you want to divert into a savings account some of the money that otherwise would go to extinguishing your debt, thereby building that cushion in the event some unforeseen financial trauma happens to you or your spouse?

There are no right and wrong answers here. As I said, everyone has their own notion of how to manage their money. But these are the questions two partners must ask of one another so that they can begin to effectively confront their debts, whether that's new debt they're taking on after marriage or pre-marital debt they're trying to pay off. Because while you can put retirement savings on auto-pilot (a 401(k) plan or automatic deposits into an IRA) and never worry with it again, you can't do the same with the money you owe your creditors. You must proactively engage with your debt or risk that it consumes your finances and destabilizes your marriage.

This is the insidious side effect of debt: If you let it, debt builds over time into an obligation that can become so large that you lose perspective and, ultimately, control of your financial life. Too many couples allow themselves to use credit cards as a supplement to their income. They receive a card with a credit limit of, say, $15,000, and they see that as a funding mechanism for a lifestyle beyond their financial means. And because their paychecks can't afford this lifestyle to begin with, the debt grows, and grows . . . and grows. That's when the mental tricks take over. When your debt gets to be large enough, then suddenly the next incremental expense you want to accrue seems irrelevant.

Here's what I mean: It's Friday night. The week has been much too long. You dread the thought of going home to cook and clean, and all you really want is to plop your butt into a seat at a restaurant and have someone else cater to your hunger and thirst. You call your spouse. You make a date. And you both arrive at your favorite barbecue and blues joint just after work for some properly smoked brisket, a few cold beers and a night of music. The tab might reach $75 with the tip, maybe $100. But, look, you're already carrying more then $22,000 of credit card debt on three different cards, and though you're struggling to pay them down, you think to yourself, "What difference is another $100 going to make?"

That's the beginning of the end.

You're digging a hole deeper and deeper because you think there's no way out of the hole to begin with. As the debt grows, so will the tension that invades your marriage. You end up buffeted by such intense financial pressure that you're incapable of living the life you both want. Every discretionary dollar you earn—maybe even more— is earmarked for some creditor. You and your spouse feel increasingly confined and mad at one another. This is not what you signed up for. Yet, here it is.

Look back to the point that lead you to a lender in the first place. Why are you here?

GOOD DEBT, BAD DEBT

Mention the word "debt" and people instantly recall negative images like, say, debtor's prison or debt counseling or debt problems or drowning in debt. Generally speaking, debt is looked upon in a bad way. Despite perceptions, though, not all debt is bad. Indeed, debt itself is a just a tool that, if used properly, can help you live a better life.

To that end, there is good debt and there is bad debt, and the goal of any couple is to use the good debt to improve the family's life, while limiting the ability of the bad debt to destroy that life.

- **Good Debt:**
  A mortgage on an affordable house, which is one of the leading ways families build wealth over time; a loan on an affordable car, which provides the means for reaching better-paying jobs;

student loans to pay for a college degree, which creates better opportunities to earn substantially greater income. In effect, good debt improves your life permanently.

- **Bad Debt:**
  Auto leases, since they're generally taken out on cars you otherwise can't afford; home-equity loans or lines of credit in which the proceeds are used to fund a vacation or some other discretionary purchase; any consumer expenses for which you allow the balance to roll over from month to month. In effect, bad debt does improve your life, but only temporarily—at best.

Couples find themselves overloaded by bad debt because they fail to practice financial self-restraint, succumbing to the temptation of bad debt. It's an easy occurrence in an age when credit cards and debit cards and keychain fobs that you swipe in front of the reader at the gas-station mini-mart allow you to spend without ever having to physically touch a dollar bill. It's all too easy to accumulate debt.

But why do you?

For many people it starts with an "I want" psychosis. They lose contact with, or fail to accept the boundaries of, their financial reality because those boundaries don't jibe with who they think they are or what they think they deserve, and it all crumbles from there. So what if I only make $30,000 a year? I should have a BMW convertible because I work hard and I've always wanted one and it will make me feel better about myself and I'll just cut back my spending elsewhere to afford the $450-a-month lease.

That's the addictive nature of bad debt. Like illicit drugs, it alters your mood by allowing you to mask through spending the unmet needs elsewhere in your life. Like drugs, its effects are instantaneous and potent, and you keep returning because debt lets you have what you want now, evoking feelings of contentment or happiness, though those feelings are always fleeting. Like drugs, debt has the power to ultimately cleave apart a relationship, and if that relationship is your marriage, then it leaves as its waste a trail of financial destruction— sometimes marital destruction—and obligations you're both responsible for.

Of course, it doesn't have to be this way. You are in control of the credit card in your wallet. You're the one who says no to the auto lease for the car you otherwise couldn't afford with cash or a car loan. You're the one who decides it's wiser to leave the equity in your home instead of drawing it out through a line of credit to pay for vacations and consumer purchases. Indeed, the savviest couples financially are those who recognize that, at the end of the day, debt should serve only one purpose: to help you and your spouse build a better life— not a better lifestyle. A better lifestyle that is sustainable can only come when you create wealth through savings and investing, or as you parlay your education and skills into a higher paying job. Bad debt will certainly allow you to live the high life for a little while, but only a little while. When the ultimate bills come due—and they always do—the lifestyle you've built evaporates as if but a dream . . . and, in effect, it really was.

Hew to your debt philosophy and you won't face that nightmare.

Just Say No . . . to Merging Your Debt

This will no doubt sound hypocritical, given that I've spent all these words up until now talking about bringing your financial life together as a single unit. But now I'm reversing myself.

When it comes to debt, you don't want to immediately decide to merge what you each owe. At some point, that might serve the family well. But early on, it's a bad idea.

Many couples will get married, and do one of two things: They either put the other on their individual credit card as a joint account

Divided We Stand. United We Fall.

You've already read about the benefits of merging individual checking accounts into a joint account. That can nurture financial intimacy and, ultimately, help create family wealth. Forget, though, that I ever mentioned this concept of unity when it comes to the individual debts you each might bring into a marriage.

Never officially co-mingle your consumer debt in any way, such as combining individual credit card balances on a new, joint credit card. Doing so can affect you credit scores negatively, making it more difficult or more costly to obtain credit later. For example, you both have credit cards now, each with credit limits of $15,000. You carry a balance of $3,000, your partner $10,000. Lenders look at something called your credit-to-debt ratio, which is basically your available credit in relation to your current debt load. So in our example, your $3,000 balance equates to a debt load of 20%, while your spouse's $10,000 represents a debt load of about 67%, high, but there's still breathing room.

But you two decide to consolidate both credit card balances on a joint card, and cancel your individual cards. Your new card also has a credit limit of $15,000, and you've transferred $13,000 onto it. Suddenly the credit agencies that monitor this stuff think your family is drowning in debt because your debt load is nearly 90%. That leaves little margin for error. So, your credit score will fall, likely precipitously, making it more expensive for you to borrow to pay for big-ticket items like houses and cars.

My point is that you can certainly help one another repay the individual debt brought into the marriage, and that can be part of your debt philosophy. Just don't merge your debt.

Now, just to confuse the situation slightly, know that joining together on some pre-existing debt, such as a mortgage, is fine. If one of you already owns a house when you two get married, adding the new spouse to the mortgage isn't a problem. It won't impact the rate you pay because the mortgage is already in place, and it's not going to affect your credit score, unless you default on the payments.

holder, or they opt to apply for a low-interest rate and proceed to combine their individual credit card debt on the new card. Neither is terribly smart, really, despite what you might read on some wedding-planning or newlywed websites. Here's why: You're each suddenly responsible for the other's past mistakes.

Let's say one of you has some meaningful level of debt on your card. That debt is your sole responsibility. If you default on it, the creditor can only come after you since your spouse had nothing to do with accumulating the charges. But as soon as the spouse signs on as joint account holder, or as soon as you two decide to consolidate all your debt onto a single card in both your names, all bets are off. Now, every last penny is the responsibility of either of you.

Imagine if the marriage doesn't last that long—maybe only a few months, as some do. Now you're on the hook for repaying purchases you had nothing to do with and that were made possibly years before you even knew the person who is now your ex.

Or let's assume the marriage doesn't fail. Instead, the spouse who had the large load of debt defaults on the account without your knowledge. If you've signed on as a joint account holder, then your credit history is affected. That, in turn, can have expensive ramifications on the family in ways you might not even consider.

So many transactions these days are based on credit scores. Some utilities companies look at credit scores, as do some insurers. If your credit history looks sketchy—and a default will certainly do that—you'll be paying higher interest rates on the mortgage you obtain, the car you buy, possibly even the insurance you get. You can avoid this by keeping your individual debt separate, and by keeping your name off of credit cards you didn't apply for yourself.

Now, there is a smarter way to combine your debt without actually combining your debt. First off, keep your credit cards separate as you both work to pay off whatever debt you've each collected individually through the years. But don't do it alone. Instead, help each other extinguish the balance by earmarking part of your monthly discretionary income for debt repayment. Once you've eliminated the debt on those individual cards (a process that will naturally improve your credit score) then you apply for a jointly held, low-rate credit card that you will each use for all purchases going forward. Under this strategy, you are effectively taking on each other's individual debt—and helping one another pay off the balance—without legally obligating yourself to the other person's account.

Paper vs. Plastic: Cash vs. Credit

Few things in life these days require money in its physical form. Indeed, many, particularly in the age of the Internet, actually require a credit card. Little wonder, then, that we've come to rely so heavily on plastic to live our lives. But credit is that mythological Damoclesian Sword. You live blithely beneath it, never realizing the dangers, hanging so precariously above your head, that credit can inflict on finances and a relationship until it's well too late.

In it's benign form, the use of credit to pay for a pizza is an otherwise unremarkable transaction in your week. You sign the check, you take away your pizza and you pay the tab when the statement arrives next month, when the memory of that night's pepperoni and pineapple is long forgotten. That, generally speaking, is healthy credit; you briefly borrowed someone else's money—namely, the creditor's—to afford a small purchase your budget could handle, and you repaid the cost in full when due.

In its malignant form, however, the use of credit to pay for a pizza is an otherwise unremarkable transaction in your descent into turmoil and discord and, possibly, bankruptcy and even divorce. Yes, credit is so powerful that it can cause divorce. That's not hyperbole. In my job as a reporter, I've interviewed people who were married for years, only to find that their husband or wife was racking up huge debts on secret credit cards that, when the bills ultimately came to light, destroyed the family. And the bills always come to light. It's only a matter of when, never if.

That pizza, in the moment, represents the evening's meal. But when you fail to pay it off in full when due—meaning you allow part of your monthly credit charges to roll over to the next month and beyond—and continue to pile more charges on your card, you are compounding a problem. You have a debt you're responsible for, a debt that is accumulating interest, additional money you must pay. And as that debt sits on your balance, you will no doubt use your credit card to buy more pizzas the next month, or burgers or beers or gasoline or furniture or whatever, some of which will roll over again, accruing more interest, before you start spending again in the third month. It's a cycle of financial destruction that becomes almost impossible to escape when the size of your balance due reaches a level beyond your capacity to pay. Yet, you still have a life to live. So while almost all of your discretionary income is earmarked to pay your credit card bills, you keep signing away on new charges to keep up your standard of living. Ultimately the torture doesn't end until you've maxed out your available credit so that even the minimum payments exceed your financial resources each month; creditors are calling you at home, at work and on your mobile number; and the only recourse you see is filing for bankruptcy to try to stop the hemorrhaging.

There are ways to deal with credit before it consumes your finances, and the most effective way is to live by the old-school rule that cash is king. I'm not going to make some Luddite plea that you cut up all your credit cards and revert to a cash-only economy. That's entirely impractical in a modern world. Nevertheless, putting $20 on a credit card and spending the last $20 bill in your wallet stir two entirely different emotions that you need to tap into. On a credit card you spend almost mindlessly, it's not real money you're dispensing, just your signature, so you don't feel the pain. Spending the actual cash, though, makes you think. Do I really want to use my last $20 this way? If I do, I have to go to the ATM to get more money to afford lunch later. Can I skip this purchase and make this money last longer?

Try this experiment together to get a true sense of just how power ful this cash vs. credit argument really is: For two consecutive trips to the supermarket—major trips, when you load up on all the supplies you'll need for some period—shop using credit one time and cash the other. When you make the trip with cash, do not take your credit card along; go with only the cash you've budgeted for the groceries. With each trip, buy as you normally would, picking up those spur-of-the-moment purchases when some item catches your eye.

Here's what's going to happen: When you shop with the credit card, you're going to feel freer to overspend. You're not consciously overspending, you just know in your subconscious that you can be-cause you're not limited. That box of cookies you're craving is only $3.59, and that's certainly not going to crimp your finances. And paying an extra dollar for the cereal you really want instead of the cheaper brand? So what!

The beautiful reality of the human mind is its unbounded abil-ity to compartmentalize. You spend that extra money on the cookie aisle, and that extra dollar on the cereal aisle, and by the time you've made it to the dairy case on the other side of the store, a dozen other impulse purchases are in your basket and you don't recognize that their combined additional cost is $50 or more. Why? Because each one has been compartmentalized and effectively neutered. You see the individual cost of each item at the moment you decide to buy it, but each item is individually affordable in that moment so it has no impact. When you get to the next item, it's not like you're thinking, "OK, I added $3.59 a minute ago, and I'm adding an additional dollar, so I've overspent by nearly $5 already." You're thinking, "It's only a dollar more. I can afford that."

Only when your basket of groceries is tallied do all those incremental costs converge as a much larger bill than you expected.

When you return to the store with a limited supply of cash on your next trip, and no credit card, you will consciously decide what you can and cannot afford based upon what you really need. You will pay attention to every price tag, you will probably keep track of the running tab in your head so you don't overshoot your limit, you will look for cheaper alternatives to certain items so that you might afford a splurge here and there, and you will walk out of the store, I promise, with change in your hand.

This simple act of trading paper for plastic has in one lesson made you a better steward of the family's money. That's why cash is king; it makes you think about what you're spending because you only have a limited supply on hand. Try the same experiment when you go to dinner. You'll be surprised at how many fewer appetizers you order, how many fewer drinks you order—and how many fewer wasted calories you consume.

The point of all of this is to get you and your spouse working together to pay attention to your use of credit. When you're both whipping out the credit card during the week for whatever sundry and necessary expenses you have, each expense is a whisper in a windstorm that you never hear. When you're paying with cash, the expense becomes the windstorm itself. You pay attention to it and you make wiser decisions about the necessity of each purchase. That's the definition of financial stewardship, and when spouses are both acting as financial stewards, you're in control of your finances and not, instead, rudderless.

Exterminating Your Debt: Small to Large

Pay attention: This is not what you think it's going to be.

You no doubt have read in numerous publications—including this book—about the need to pay off your consumer debt so that you can gain control over your financial life. True words. But I'll bet the prescription you've typically been told is to tackle first the credit card with the highest rate and biggest balance. Decent advice—it will certainly save you money over time.

But it's not necessarily the smart advice.

I've said many times in these pages that money is more than green paper. It is an emotional currency. And nowhere is that more apparent than when it comes to repaying the mounds of credit card debt that so many young couples accumulate before and after marriage. You know you need to pay them off; their overweight balances hang heavy on your finances, likely crimping your ability to pursue what you might really like, such as a new house, new car, fatter savings account. Getting from here to there, though, can seem such a daunting challenge, given the balances involved.

The key to success: Start small.

Little steps take you just as far as giant leaps; the journey just takes a little longer. To that end, concentrate your efforts on the card with the smallest balance. It doesn't matter whether this card imposes an interest rate of 2% or 20%. When you're trying to take control of your pocketbook, the goal is extinguish your debt as fast as you can. And if you see yourself making progress on a smaller balance, you will continue to feel inspired. On a card with a large balance, you're more easily deflated when, after many months, the balance still seems so insurmountable.

Look at it in terms of real numbers. Let's say you have two cards—one with a $2,000 balance at 12%; the other larded with $10,000 and a 20% interest rate. After building your budget, you realize you can afford to earmark an additional $100 a month to debt repayment. Put the sum toward the largest balance first—as many financial pundits insist you do—and after a year of principal and interest payments you still have about $8,800 remaining to repay. That's still a hefty load that can seem demoralizing after so much effort you put into paying it down.

Exterminating Your Debt: Small to Large, continued

On the card with the smaller balance, however, you've cut the amount you owe down to about $800, more than halving your original debt. You're seeing real progress and, better yet, you can see the finish line in sight. More than likely you're going to remain motivated to pay that card off, seeing your pending success as an emotional victory over a part of your life that at one point seemed unmanageable.

Once that small balance is paid off, focus your efforts on the next card in line. You'll do so knowing you can succeed because you've already proven to yourself that you can.

That's the power of small: You see your results sooner. More important, you gain confidence and build financial self-esteem.

You could pay more following this approach, because if the high-balance card also carries a high interest rate, well, then you're accumulating largest interest payments that you have to ultimately pay off. If you have the willpower to tackle the high-balance card first and not feel dejected when the amount you owe isn't shrinking as quickly as you'd like, then by all means pay off that card first.

Otherwise, think small.

Using Credit Prudently

I fully expect you'll use a credit card frequently in your life. I certainly do. And with tens of millions of credit cards scattered around, so too do your friends, neighbors and family. There's nothing wrong with that, so long as you're prudent in how you use your card. In this case, prudent means that you won't charge to your credit card more than the family's monthly, discretionary income can afford to pay off. The moment you spend on credit more money than you know you have coming in, you are, by definition, living beyond your means and using high-interest money to pay for a lifestyle you otherwise can't afford. Not good. That marks the point at which your financial troubles begin.

To prevent such problems, you need to determine as a couple the answer to two questions:

1. What Expenses Are Worthy of Credit?

Will you sign for everyday expenses like fast-food meals and groceries, or will you use your credit only for larger expenses like furniture?

Putting everyday expenses on a credit card, while certainly not bad, can result in monthly statements larger than you expect because, unless you keep track of every credit card receipt—and few people do it's easy to forget about these run-of-the-mill expenses accumulated during the month. But it's exactly those expenses that add up and drain away your money, leaving you feeling like you can't get ahead.

If you opt to put only big-ticket items on the card, will you have the money to pay it off at the end of the month, or will you float the cost for a few months? Will you curtail discretionary spending while this charge is on your balance so that you have the money necessary to pay back the cost in no more than two or three months?

The worst strategy you can pursue, and it's pursued far too frequently, is to buy some expensive item and continue to spend as usual on run-of-the-mill purchases. Do this and you end up spending more than your paycheck can afford—and you never build wealth, blowing your budget. What you need in this situation is a payoff plan so that this big-ticket charge doesn't hang around on your credit card for months and months, adding additional interest payments to your cost.

2. How Will You Repay the Charges?

Do you plan to carry a balance from month to month or will you pay the balance in full?

In terms of debt, this area is where stress is most likely to enter into your relationship. A large bill arriving in the mailbox each month can be enough to send one or the both of you into fits of frustration, maybe even panic over how to afford the cost when there are so many other bills that must be paid as well. Tension emerges and the arguments and fights begin.

The accumulation of debt can be a very stressful affair for some people, since it can create feelings of financial insecurity or anxiety. Find out how your partner feels about credit card debt so that you can avoid these instances. Will either of you freak out over a large credit card statement? What defines "large" in your world? And will you panic if a balance rolls over from month to month to month? The concerns and worries that underlie these questions aren't easily whitewashed, and they are cumulative, just like the debt itself. The stress that exists this month is compounded when the next bill arrives and the balance is even higher. So you need a payoff plan that you both can adhere to help temper the level of family financial stress.

If you agree the family will pay off the charges monthly then, obviously, you can't go spending beyond your ability to pay. Doing so will lead to the frustration that causes conflict. If you find you do have to spend beyond your means—I said "have to," not "want to"—at least talk about the expense first to prepare the other for what's coming, and, at the same time, to lay out the plan for repaying the overrun.

If you plan to carry a balance, or need to for whatever reason, you absolutely must have a plan in place to cut back on the amount of additional debt you take on each month. Carrying a balance requires allocating a larger portion of your discretionary income to servicing this debt. That means you have to trim your spending each month to allow for larger credit card payments. Ideally what you'd want is to have enough paycheck left over each month to repay your credit card charges for the month, plus an additional amount to pay down some of the debt you're already carrying on the card.

Know What You Spend During the Month

Your primary budgetary goal is to keep your credit card charges within the bounds of your discretionary income. As challenging as that can be for a single person, the hurdles are magnified in a marriage because now there are two people involved. That complicates matters. Unless you never leave one another's side, you two will obviously make individual spending decisions during the course of your day that the other won't know about at the moment and that you can easily forget about by the time you return home.

For that reason, partners need to keep each other apprised of the expenses they each put on the card so that those individual charges don't surprise you when they're lumped together on your bill each month. This gets to the communication issue that is so crucial to successfully managing money as a couple. The more you talk, the more open you are about how the money comes and goes, the better you're able to remain within the borders of the budget you two establish. In turn, that will allow you to save and invest to build the wealth that leads to financial security, and keep you on track to spending your money in the ways that make you most happy, meaning spending on what's most important to you.

Even if you operate with individual credit cards, the family needs some mechanism for knowing how much money it's obligated to repay at the end of the month so that the expenses never outstrip the income.

There are a numerous ways to accomplish this, including the use of financial software programs where you input each charge and you can track your spending by a zillion different categories, if you want. You can also make it a point to review your credit card statement online during the month, since the charges will show up there quickly, often the same day.

But, actually, the most effective approach is the simplest, requiring nothing more high-tech than a pencil: Keep a running tally of your credit card charges during the month on a piece of paper stuck to the refrigerator door. This way both of you to see at a glance exactly how much has already been spent on the card for the month so that you're always cognizant of the growing size of the charges. When you see that number continually rising, you will instinctively reevaluate those minor purchases that conspire each month to jack up your credit card balance.

I know this sounds like drudgery—and, honestly, it might feel like that at first. But soon enough it will become second nature to you, requiring little time at all, and you will get to a point where you don't need to constantly track your credit card expenses because you end up using your card more wisely, thinking twice about those throwaway purchases you make everyday. Ultimately you will see a smaller credit card balance each month.

Home Is Where the Heart Is

The desire for "home" may be the most primeval urge we have as a couple. Nothing says nest like your own house, a place that provides shelter, a place where you can close the door and be who you are without the world watching, where you can paint the walls as you wish, make all the racket you want without worrying about neighbors, raise a family and get out in your yard and dig around on a piece of dirt that you physically own. But this notion of "home" also represents perhaps the biggest financial mistake married couples make. So enamored are they with some particular house that they end up biting off more than their wallet can chew. It tastes good for a while, but if ultimately you have to spit it out, the aftertaste can be quite bitter.

Look no further than the imploding housing market of 2007 and 2008 for proof. Exceedingly low interest rates in the early part of the

Death by Minimum Payment

Never, ever pay the minimum payment due on a credit card.

Never.

Do so, and you'll be trapped in credit card hell, spending more dollars than you ever imagined for a period of time that can cover your entire working career.

Consider this example: You ring up a $12,000 balance on your MasterCard in college, then decide after graduation you'll never use it again and that you'll just pay it off over time making the minimum payments. Sure, no one would likely do it this way—probably—but this is just for the sake of shock value. This card has a 14% interest rate (not unreasonable), and, like many, requires a minimum payment of 2% of the monthly balance.

How long will it take to repay the debt, and how much money will you actually send to the credit card company?

Time spent: 46½ years.

Money sent: More than $35,000, of which $23,000, or nearly double the original charges, is interest.

Priceless. Right?

Double up on the minimum and you cut your repayment schedule to 14 years and the amount you ultimately repay to $18,000. Certainly, your family income may preclude doubling up each month, and that's understandable when you have a big balance that results in big monthly minimums. But whatever you do, pay more than the minimum so that you shrink your balance as quickly as possible. And when you come into extra cash through bonuses or overtime or even family gifts of money, put some or all of that cash toward your balance. It will save you thousands of dollars in the long term.

Now, there's a school of thought that believes that carrying a certain amount of semi-permanent debt on a credit card is healthy because it basically allows you to pay your life forward. You live for now knowing you can pay the piper later in life when your salary takes a big leap or larger bonuses start rolling in. I've never seen the logic in that.

The only instance where it's necessary to carry a credit card balance for any period of time is in the support of your health. If you must see a doctor or decade mixed with lax lending standards, a host of complicated mortgages, and a lack of discipline on the part of borrowers created one of the worst financial calamities since the Great Depression. Those complicated mortgages that made homeownership easy early on turned malicious as their interest rates reset higher and higher, doubling and tripling monthly payments, driving unprepared homeowners to the brink.

An oversupply of homes pushed them into the abyss. Demand for housing in those early years of the decade spurred a building boom that ultimately created far too many houses for buyers to absorb. At that point, home prices, which had only known one direction—up— rolled over, leaving homeowners struggling with those rising mortgage payments even as the value of the house was falling. Many found themselves upside down in their mortgage—meaning they owed more on their house than the house was worth. As such, they couldn't refinance out of the whirlpool they were stuck in.

The result was one of the most rapid escalations in foreclosures the country has ever seen.

Often couples find themselves in such difficult straits because one or the other, or both, fall in love with a house and can't see themselves living anywhere else, even if the house is beyond their means. The conversation that leads to this event almost always sounds like some version of this:

"We were only looking to spend $175,000 . . ."

"I know, but this is only $30,000 more. We can swing that, right? I love this house. I can really see us living here and being happy."

"I don't know. Can we really afford this? Thirty-thousand dollars is a lot more than we expected to pay."

"But this is the perfect house for us. It's the nicest one we've seen. We'd probably spend $30,000 to fix up the other houses we saw, so it's all the same, really. We can make this work. We can cut back on eating out and I can work some overtime every month. We can make it work.."

"It *is* the perfect house. And I'm supposed to get a raise next year, so that will give us more income. Maybe we can make it work . . ."

You've just talked yourself into a potential nightmare. Buying too much house has proven the downfall of many a couple. Houses stand for so much more than a place to live. They speak to who we are or who we think we are. The neighborhood we choose determines the schools our kids attend, our commute to and from work and the crowd of people we associate with. It says something about how well we're doing financially, and leads those around us to make assumptions— right or wrong—about our station in life. As such, home buying is as much an emotional decision as a financial one.

Therein lies the problem. In making what is likely to be the biggest purchase of their lives, couples far too frequently allow the emotion to drive their decision, undermining what is best for the family financially. Yes, you can stretch to afford that perfect house that costs $30,000 more, but what happens when you're unhappy having to cut out all your entertainment expenses to afford the note? Will you still be happy to come home night after night to cook another meal when all you want is to go a restaurant, if only you had the money? What happens if the overtime you expected doesn't materialize to the degree you expected? What happens if that raise doesn't come through? When you believe in magic, you end up hoodwinked.

The ultimate tragedy with too much house is that it precludes you from attaining other goals, whether financial or personal.

Think about it: If you're sending a mortgage company 50% or more of your take-home pay every month—on top of your costs for groceries, electricity, gasoline and other necessities—you're not going to have many, if any, discretionary funds remaining to pursue other wants, such as those meals out or, more importantly, saving for the future.

And if money issues weren't bad enough, the perfect house debate can quickly devolve into a contentious battle between spouses. One wants that white-picket-fence dream this house represents, while the other sees only the huge costs and the impact the price tag and monthly mortgage payment will have on the family's wealth and ability to live comfortably. So one of you argues with your heart, the other the wallet—and you end up talking right past one another because you're each speaking a different language.

To quell such arguments before they begin, you both need to know what the family's pocketbook can truly afford.

How Much House Can You Afford?
Pre-Qualify Yourself

Before you ever call a real-estate agent, before you even shop for a house, you need to determine together how much house you two can afford so that you concentrate your house-hunting in the neighborhoods that fall comfortably into your price range. Then, consciously agree as a couple not to venture beyond that. To stanch any temptation, don't even look at houses listed more than about 10% beyond your price cap. The 10% gives you some room to look at slightly nicer homes or ones in more desirable neighborhoods.

To determine what you can afford means to effectively pre-qualify yourself for a mortgage. There are two ways to do this: based on the level of your income; or based on your current debt obligations. We'll use the same tools lenders do—the so-called front-end and back-end ratios. I know, this wades into the murky world of math, but don't be put off by the numbers and calculations; they're elementary-school easy—plus there's a worksheet to walk you through the process. More important, follow these guidelines conservatively and you'll be living within your means, the key to financial success, regardless of whether you earn $1 million a year or $50,000.

- **Front-End Ratio:**
  Your total **monthly mortgage payment**, divided by your monthly gross income. This figure should not exceed a range of between 28% and 30% of your gross income allocated to mortgage expenses, and that includes principal, interest, taxes and insurance—know as PITI. If you earn, say, $75,000 a year, or $6,250 a month, your PITI shouldn't exceed $1,875 a month (6250 x 0.30).

- **Back-End Ratio:**
  Your total **monthly debt** divided by your gross monthly income. Here, you generally want to stay in the 36% to 40% range. Pay attention, though: This is your total debt, not just your mortgage. So this incorporates credit card payments, car notes, leases, bank loans, student loans, child-support payments, alimony, tax liens and other such expenses in addition to the mortgage. With that same $6,250 in monthly gross income, your back-end total cannot exceed $2,500 (6250 x 0.40).

Use the Affordability Calculator on the next page to help you calculate all these numbers and see for yourself where you should be shopping. To be conservative, base your home purchase on the lower of the front-end and back-end ratios.

Remember that a house payment isn't just the mortgage. It's comprised of your homeowner's insurance and your property taxes, too. So, you've got to factor those into your math. Call two or three insurers and give them the details of the houses you're looking to buy, and they will calculate an annual or monthly premium. Likewise, check with the local tax assessor's office to find out the most recent year's property taxes on the houses you're researching. Knowing all of this information before you sign off on a mortgage will keep you from feeling strapped financially by a house you ultimately can't afford.

The Practice Mortgage

If either or both of you are seriously pushing for a house priced beyond your pre-qualified limit, then prepare two monthly budgets. With one, plan a budget based on an affordable house. Base the other on the more expensive house with the more expensive mortgage payment. Then, institute the harsher budget in your real finances for a while before agreeing to buy the costlier house. Limit the family's spending each month to exactly what will be available once the larger mortgage is in place.

If the expensive mortgage is, say, $1,000 and your current mortgage or rental payment is $700, then pay your note as you normally must and then take the other $300 out of your spending for the month. Stick the money in a savings account or mutual fund or even pull it out in cash and stuff it into a safe-deposit box at the bank. Just don't cheat and really use that money during the month. You need to see exactly how life will feel with the bigger mortgage in place. A dose of fiscal reality may be just enough to convince dreamers that the

Affordability Calculator

This chart will help you quickly determine how much a particular home will cost you. To use it, simply divide the house's price by 1,000, then multiply that answer by the appropriate number in the chart based on the mortgage you're pursuing. Example: You're looking at a $250,000 house, and a 30-year mortgage at 6.25%. Divide $250,000, by 1,000 to get 250. Then multiply that by $6.16 (where 6.25% and 30 years cross on the chart) and you get a monthly principal and interest payment of $1,540.

How Much House Can You Afford?

	Example	Your House
Front-End Ratio:		
Gross Monthly Income	$4,000.00	
Many lenders limit your housing expense to 30% of your gross monthly income. But change this to reflect what your lender allows. x	0.3 x	
Front-End Maximum Mortgage =	$1,200.00	
Back-End Ratio:		
Gross Monthly Income	$4,000.00	
Lenders generally limit your total-debt payments to 40% of your gross monthly income. But change this to reflect what your lender allows. x	0.4 x	
Preliminary monthly mortgage =	$1,600.00	
Debt Obligations:		
Car Loan	$350.00	

Affordability Calculator, continued

		Example	Your House
Credit Card(s) Minimum		$100.00	
Child Support		n/a	
Student Loans		n/a	
Other		n/a	
Total Monthly Debt Payments	=	$450.00	
Back-End Maximum Mortgage: *Subtract your total monthly debt from your preliminary monthly mortgage*	=	$1,150.00	
Record the smaller of the **Front-End** or **Back-End Maximum Mortgage**		$1,150.00	
Subtract your estimated monthly taxes *(or call your tax assessor)*	−	$200.00	−
Subtract your estimated monthly insurance payment *(or call an agent for a quote)*	−	$100.00	−
Monthly Payment on which to base your purchase price	=	$850.00	
Refer to the chart on the next page to find the interest rate and mortgage you will use (i.e., 30-year, 6.5%) and divide your monthly payment by that number . . .	÷	$6.32	÷
	=	$134.49	=
. . . and then multiply the result by 1,000 to determine the amount of house you can afford.		$134,494.00	

Use this chart to determine the monthly payment, per $1,000, for various interest rates. Column 1 is for 15-year fixed-rate mortgages; Column 2 is for 30-year fixed-rate mortgages.

Rate	15-year	30-year	Rate	15-year	30-year
3%	$ 6.91	$ 4.22	7%	$ 8.99	$ 6.65
3.125%	$ 6.97	$ 4.28	7.125%	$ 9.06	$ 6.74
3.25%	$ 7.03	$ 4.35	7.25%	$ 9.13	$ 6.82
3.375%	$ 7.09	$ 4.42	7.375%	$ 9.20	$ 6.91
3.50%	$ 7.15	$ 4.49	7.50%	$ 9.27	$ 6.99
3.625%	$ 7.21	$ 4.56	7.625%	$ 9.34	$ 7.08
3.75%	$ 7.27	$ 4.63	7.75%	$ 9.41	$ 7.16
3.875%	$ 7.33	$ 4.70	7.875%	$ 9.48	$ 7.25
4%	$ 7.40	$ 4.77	8%	$ 9.56	$ 7.34
4.125%	$ 7.46	$ 4.85	8.125%	$ 9.63	$ 7.42
4.25%	$ 7.52	$ 4.92	8.25%	$ 9.70	$ 7.51
4.375%	$ 7.59	$ 4.99	8.375%	$ 9.77	$ 7.60
4.50%	$ 7.65	$ 5.07	8.50%	$ 9.85	$ 7.69
4.625%	$ 7.71	$ 5.14	8.625%	$ 9.92	$ 7.78
4.75%	$ 7.78	$ 5.22	8.75%	$ 9.99	$ 7.87
4.875%	$ 7.84	$ 5.29	8.875%	$10.07	$ 7.96
5%	$ 7.91	$ 5.37	9%	$10.14	$ 8.05
5.125%	$ 7.97	$ 5.44	9.125%	$10.22	$ 8.14
5.25%	$ 8.04	$ 5.52	9.25%	$10.29	$ 8.23
5.375%	$ 8.10	$ 5.60	9.375%	$10.37	$ 8.32
5.50%	$ 8.17	$ 5.68	9.50%	$10.44	$ 8.41
5.625%	$ 8.24	$ 5.76	9.625%	$10.52	$ 8.50
5.75%	$ 8.30	$ 5.84	9.75%	$10.59	$ 8.59
5.875%	$ 8.37	$ 5.92	9.875%	$10.67	$ 8.68
6%	$ 8.44	$ 6.00	10%	$10.75	$ 8.78
6.125%	$ 8.51	$ 6.08	10.125%	$10.82	$ 8.87
6.25%	$ 8.57	$ 6.16	10.25%	$10.90	$ 8.96
6.375%	$ 8.64	$ 6.24	10.375%	$10.98	$ 9.05
6.50%	$ 8.71	$ 6.32	10.50%	$11.05	$ 9.15
6.625%	$ 8.78	$ 6.40	10.625%	$11.13	$ 9.24
6.75%	$ 8.85	$ 6.49	10.75%	$11.21	$ 9.33
6.875%	$ 8.92	$ 6.57	10.875%	$11.29	$ 9.43

dream house can instead feel like a nightmare when so few dollars remain to pursue discretionary expenses and the ability to save money and build some financial security into your life is so compromised.

If you are the spouse pressing for the pricey home, realize that the size of your mortgage is truly a big deal. If you can't afford rent for an apartment, fine; you can pretty easily relocate to cheaper digs, cutting back your housing costs in the process. You're not facing the level of emotional and financial trauma you struggle with if you can't afford the monthly note for your house.

All manner of hurdles stop you from packing up the dishes and leaving behind a house for a cheaper place to live. Key among them: the mortgage itself. You can abandon your house, but you can never shake the mortgage. It follows your every move, a legal shadow tethered to you until the balance is paid in full. Don't pay, and the lender will foreclose, take possession of your house, sell it at auction, pocket the money required to repay the debt and fees, and return to you whatever sum remains—and often what remains is nothing. You end up losing every penny of equity you put into this home.

How realistic is this, really? Well, consider the events of 2007 and 2008. For several years during the early part of the decade, interest rates where unnaturally low and lenders introduced all manner of unconventional mortgages to entice new-home buyers. In many instances these mortgages were structured so that people who otherwise could not afford a house were able to buy one. To make it work, lenders allowed these buyers to purchase homes with no money down, no proof of income, and using mortgages that offered ultra-low introductory interest rates. Couples paid little attention to the fine print, instead excited by the prospect of a mortgage that could get them into the house of their dreams.

And then the bottom fell out. Many homeowners began falling behind in their mortgage payments because they couldn't afford those payments to begin with. In other cases the mortgages were tied to adjustable rates, meaning the interest rate would reset higher after a few years, pushing up the mortgage payment. For many borrowers, the recalculated payments were way beyond their ability to pay. The net effect: A record number of foreclosures rocked the housing industry.

Now, assuming you don't want to go through foreclosure and, therefore, don't abandon the house when the mortgage becomes too much to handle, you'll have to sell your home. In more normal times, when the decision to sell is entirely yours, that's traumatic enough. The trauma is magnitudes worse when you're selling not because you willingly want to leave, but because financial pressures are forcing you into this transaction. You'll generally need to sell in a hurry to avoid foreclosure, and that almost always means you take a haircut on the price, maybe a big haircut. You're giving up a potentially large amount of equity that you otherwise might keep if you had more time to market the house. Perhaps the worst development in all of this, though, is that as your financial life slides off the cliff, it invariably pulls your relationship with it because of the magnitude of the emotions involved—everything from angst and anger to sadness, fury and disappointment. That can extract a heavy toll from a marriage. Certainly, you can recover from such an event, but it can also destroy the relationship forever.

And to think it all started with beautiful dreams of that perfect house . . . priced too far beyond your limit.

Again, it doesn't have to be this way; remember that. You are in control of your spending. You, as a couple, singularly determine how much house you can honestly afford. You can do it the emotional way and face the struggles that ensue. Or you can do it the logical way and agree to adhere to a price limit that you know you can live with. If you really can work all those additional overtime hours, and you really do get that raise you were expecting next year, excellent. Save those extra dollars every month instead of spending them, and when you can afford it, go buy that perfect house. At that point, you will have earned it and your financial life won't suffer.

Beware the Magical Mortgage

So how do you know if you're buying too much house?

Here's a clue: If your lender cannot qualify you for the home of your dreams using a traditional, fixed-rate mortgage and, instead, talks to you about considering adjustable-rate or interest-only mortgages, you're on the verge of living beyond your means.

That's not to say any mortgages other than the traditional 15- or 30-year fixed-rate mortgages are bad. They're not. Savvy homebuyers who understand the risks of non-traditional mortgages use them with great effect as a way to essentially "play" the mortgage market for a relatively short period at a time when interest rates are flat or headed down. But the vast bulk of homeowners are more concerned with creating a home than worrying about interest-rate movements, and these magical mortgages are generally trouble waiting to happen.

Indeed, magical mortgages were at the heart of the housing disaster in 2007 and 2008. Borrowers did not understand the complexity of the mortgages they agreed to. They did not understand that those mortgages would recast at some point and, in doing so, would raise the monthly payments by large amounts—so large in some cases that the monthly payment exceeded the family's ability to pay. The only fact buyers seemed to understand was that these mortgages started off cheap and, thus, allowed homeowners to afford houses that were clearly beyond their means to begin with.

So before you pursue a magical mortgage—and before you potentially put yourself in a precarious financial condition—understand exactly what you're getting into. In most cases, you'll want to steer clear of these products.

Adjustable-Rate Mortgages

Known as ARMs, these mortgages generally start off with an affordable, teaser interest rate that is either slightly below or well below prevailing fixed-rate mortgages. That's what makes them so enticing: The lower rate obviously means a smaller monthly payment.

The teaser rate remains in effect for anywhere from one to ten years. When that period ends, the rate potentially readjusts, depending upon interest-rate movements in the broader economy at that time. If interest rates are higher than when you signed for the mortgage, your rate—and your payment—is headed up. If interest rates are unchanged, your mortgage rate stays the same for the time being. If rates are down, your interest rate could fall or remain unchanged.

Once the readjustments begin, they recur annually, though some particularly aggressive ARMs reset more frequently. ARMs have caps that limit how much they can readjust annually, as well as how much they can readjust over the life of the mortgage. That might be empty consolation, though, if the readjusted rate means your mortgage payment moves far past your ability to pay. That's the big worry you need to consider.

If you borrow $225,000 to buy the average American home, using an ARM initially set at 5.75% for five years, which can then readjust by as much as two percentage points annually and as much as six percentage points over the life of the mortgage, then at some point your mortgage payment could be tied to a rate of 11.75%. In such a situation, your initial mortgage payment (the principal and interest, not taxes and homeowner's insurance) will be $1,313 a month, but could surge to nearly $2,140 within seven years. Can you live with the risk of a payment that could jump that dramatically?

Sure, you can always refinance the loan when the teaser period is over, but if you see that as a good plan, then it's largely because rates have already moved higher and you don't want to get caught by the first readjustment. Only, by then, 30-year, fixed-rate mortgages already reflect the higher interest rates and, thus, no matter how you look at it, your mortgage payment will be headed higher.

If you're ever considering an ARM, do your wallet a favor and ask your lender to run a worst-case scenario so that you can see exactly how your payments might change over time. Then, you and your spouse need to ask yourselves if you can live with the possibilities. If you can't, then avoid the ARM to begin with.

Interest-Only Mortgages

A typical mortgage payment includes both the principal and interest; these mortgages, often called IO mortgages, require only monthly interest payments for a set number of years, usually five or ten. After that period, principal payments kick in. In essence, the IO mortgage gives you a break early on by keeping your payments in the early years more affordable, but does so by compressing your principal payments into a shorter window, say 20 or 25 years instead of 30 years. That means the mortgage balance remains unchanged for all the years you're paying the interest portion since you are not paying down the principal amount you borrowed.

The net effect to your wallet happens when the interest-only period ends and you must begin paying down the principal: Your monthly mortgage payments take a noticeable leap higher.

The supposed benefit for homeowners is that the lower monthly note in the early years makes it easier to qualify for a house. Larger payments arrive, in theory at least, after you have presumably earned nice raises at work or job-hopped your way to a bigger salary, making the higher payment just as affordable as the lower payment was. If all works as planned, well, then, the interest-only gambit was a good decision since it allowed you to buy a home you otherwise couldn't afford at that moment.

But if life doesn't go as planned, if your salary doesn't move up as quickly as you expected, or you lose your job, or you can't find a higher paying job, or you now have three kids instead of one, then the bump up in the monthly payments can be a financial trauma that strains you checkbook and your marriage. And for the record, large-scale financial stress—such as the kind that occurs when your house suddenly becomes unaffordable—always finds a way to invade a marriage.

Here's how to make the pain even worse: Seek out an adjustable-rate IO mortgage, known as an Option ARM. This is the equivalent of playing Russian roulette—with multiple bullets. Not only do you face the guaranteed bump-up when the principal payments begin, you face the even scarier prospect that interest rates will surge, driving the interest portion of your payment markedly higher just as your principal payments rise.

Options ARMs get their name from the fact that you have the *option* each month to pay a traditional monthly payment (principal and interest), an interest-only payment, or a "minimum payment" that is typically less than the interest-only payments. From month to month you can choose what payment option fits your finances best.

But be fully warned: These can be exceedingly dangerous to your wealth. So many hidden caveats lurk in the fine print, and they can be so confusing, that you can mortgage yourself into a world of hurt without even realizing what just happened. One small example: Most folks don't realize that the low minimum payment, which can be half the size of the interest-only payment, means your principal is actually *rising*. You might have borrowed $250,000 to buy the house, but your mortgage balance after year one of paying only the minimum has risen to nearly $260,000.

All the while you've been paying your mortgage, you're actually digging a deeper hole. This is known as negative amortization, and it can bite you hard in a situation where home prices have softened, the economy is tepid and your house is now worth less than the mortgage balance. You're underwater, and if you're forced to sell your house for whatever reason, you'll have to come up with additional money on top of the sales price just to pay back the mortgage—not a situation anyone wants to be in.

Thus, for the bulk of homebuyers, IO mortgages—and Option ARMs, in particular—are an unadulterated gamble that is best to avoid.

CHAPTER 5

HOUSEHOLD SAVINGS: INVESTING FOR TOMORROW

The future promises to be a scary place, at least in terms of money.

The reason? The very large dollars your future will cost, what with two or three decades in retirement to worry about and the price tag for your kid's college. Husbands and wives sees those dollar signs and each have their own ways of thinking about, planning for or avoiding them. That process is rife with potential conflict. Think about this: You recognize what the expenses of the future are going to cost and, concerned about how to pay for it, you seek to save every penny you can; your spouse, meanwhile, wants to avoid the paralyzing thought that your child's college bills could exceed $100,000 and retirement will require $1 million or more, and would just rather live life now by spending on trips and cars and houses the very dollars you would rather be saving.

Or maybe there's a huge risk-tolerance gap. You're a gambler, willing to assume risks necessary for the big score. Your spouse is a financial teetotaler, unwilling to shoulder the responsibility if your gamble goes awry and leaves the family hard up for money and struggling financially. Tell me that's not going to spark some tension.

Thus it is that even as you worry about future shocks destined to rock your wallet, you face the stress of managing the marital strife that all too often rides shotgun with these decisions.

The aim, then, of saving and investing isn't just the savings and investing. Success is learning to deal with that strife so that you and your partner move toward a unified agenda that has you both pulling in the same direction—or at least getting to the point where you both say, "I can live with that." Neither spouse should feel unhappy or, in particular, insecure with how the family's money is invested for the future. And both partners must know—*absolutely must know*—the direction in which the family is headed with its savings and investment scheme. Otherwise, what's the point? You spend your life together only to reach some destination in the future that only one of you has an interest in? That's a marriage doomed to failure or, at the very least, perpetual unhappiness.

The biggest matter on the minds of younger newlyweds—the Gen X and Gen Y crowd—is likely to be affording a child's education. Statistics collected by financial services companies bear this out. Younger couples save for retirement as best they can in a 401(k) plan and take the view that if it gets them to where they need to be, great; if not, well, they can worry about that much later. First and foremost is building a big enough educational account to pay for Junior's college one day. That makes some sense, at least chronologically speaking, since Junior's college days will arrive before retirement.

In practical terms, though, it's not the best approach for a variety of reasons we'll get to in a moment. But since saving for college is where younger couples are mentally, that's where we'll start . . .

College Savings 101

First-time parents get so wrapped up in preparing everything just so for baby's arrival. New crib. New nursery. New stroller. New college-savings account. It's not hard to find a soon-to-be mom or dad who has already scoped out the savings options and begun funding an account, before the kid even pops into the world.

That's understandable, given the bulging costs of a university degree. In the 2007–08 school year, the average public university charged nearly $6,200 for students who qualify for in-state fees. Factor in tuition inflation of 6% a year (and tuition inflation has been running slightly higher than that, actually), and you're looking at a four-year outlay exceeding $27,000. That doesn't include room and board, by the way. At the private-school level, you're talking about inflation-adjusted costs right at $100,000 for a degree. And, remember, this is in 2007 dollars. If your child is a newborn, or not even of this world just yet, you have to think about college costs 18 to 20 years from now—which for a state school means four-year costs of roughly $90,000. I won't even horrify your senses with the cost of a private-school degree two decades ahead.

Yes, you will certainly—hopefully—be earning over the years more money through promotions and pay raises, but college costs have been rising much faster than the overall cost of living, and no matter how you look at it, tuition payments are often a source of financial stress for families.

But there are ways to make this more manageable.

First—and this is perhaps one of the bigger divides between couples—you don't have to save every last dime needed to cover college costs. Nor must you pay every last dime of tuition for your child. To many parents, that's heresy. But let's think through both of those assertions:

1. You don't have to save every dime.

The good thing about college tuition—assuming there is a good thing—is that it generally arrives during your peak earning years. As such, you'll be able to pull a meaningful chunk of dollars right out of your income stream each semester. Therefore, you don't need to struggle in your early years, when your paychecks are markedly smaller, to save all those dollars you think you'll need.

Moreover, the academic world is swimming in scholarship dollars.

As of 2008, there are roughly $3 billion available to students through all manner of organizations, associations and state and federal governments. A big part of that stash goes unclaimed each year for any number of reasons. That means your child has many opportunities to earn a scholarship to help you afford college. Also, there are grants and work-study programs on campus, as well as jobs off campus, to defray all or part of the costs.

If all else fails, there are loans widely available from public and private lenders that your child can pursue. You'll even find loans for parents to help their kids pay for college.

Everything you need to know about scholarships and loans is at www.fastweb.com and www.salliemae.com.

2. You don't have to pay every dime.

The reality of most American financial lives is that not enough dollars exist in the average paycheck to do everything you want/need to do. You have to choose what's most important. And to be blunt about it, what should be most important isn't funding your child's college education at the expense of your own retirement.

Unlike your child's collegiate career, no one will ever offer you a scholarship or grant to live your retirement. You can, of course, work through your retirement to make ends meet, if that's really how you want to spend the part of your life that is supposed to be substantially more carefree and kicked back.

Consider this question: What legacy do you want to give your children?

You can provide them a free ride through college, but at what cost to their own future? Here's what I mean: Without adequate retirement savings, you will potentially need your own financial assistance in retirement. That could leave you knocking on your kid's door, seeking financial handouts more than once just to afford in retirement what your nest egg can't because you put all your money into their education. And while your children may be grateful for your sacrifice, they're still likely to resent having to fund your later years with their money.

Moreover, their spouse is likely to feel put upon, leading to the exact same kinds of emotionally trying financial dustups that you seek to avoid in your own life now.

Here's a related reason you don't have to pay every dime: Your children have their entire working career to repay whatever loans are necessary to afford their education, and they're likely to have the money to do so, given that Sallie Mae, the nation's leading provider of student loans, reports that college graduates over the course of their career typically earn about $1.5 million more than non-matriculating peers.

In contrast, you won't have an entire career left to save for retirement after spending your savings on your child's education. A smarter strategy: Build a comfortable nest egg for retirement, and then, after your child is in the workforce, use whatever money you can spare to help them repay whatever loans they had to take out. That will mean just as much to them.

Where to Save for College

Lots of words have been written in many books and magazines and newspapers about the various investment options for college savings—Coverdell Education Savings Accounts, trust accounts established in your child's name, and so-called 529 College Savings Plans, named for the section of the tax code (Section 529) that grants them tax-advantaged status. Dissecting the nuances of each is well beyond the scope of this book. But in terms of bang for the buck, the 529 plans are my plan of choice.

Trust accounts, while most flexible in terms of investment options— effectively unlimited—impose tax obligations that ultimately shrink the value of the account. The Coverdell plans severely constrict the amount of money you can save annually, potentially leaving you well behind where you'd like to be, though their benefit over trust accounts is that your investment grows tax deferred and the money, when withdrawn, comes out tax free if used for qualified educational expenses.

The 529 plans offer the same tax benefit, but you can squirrel away vastly more money, allowing not just you and your partner to fund the account, but grandparents and aunts and uncles and others to contribute as well. They could all contribute to the Coverdell, too, but the contribution limits are so low for the Coverdell, just $2,000 annually in 2008 (and that begins to phase out at higher income levels), that you'd tap out the account quickly. The contribution limit on the 529 savings plan is effectively $250,000, either over time or in one lump sum. Moreover, the money in the 529 plan doesn't have to be used by any particular date. You can, in fact, change beneficiaries to another child or a grandchild, if your original beneficiary skips college, earns a free-ride through academics or sports proficiency . . . or just decides to join the circus. You can even change the beneficiary to yourself, if none of your kids use the dollars and you ultimately decide you want to go back to school at some point. With the Coverdell, the account balance must be distributed to the beneficiary (which can be changed under very limited circumstances) by the age of 30, or else the account is forcibly distributed, all earnings are taxed as ordinary income (typically the highest income-tax rates), and then penalized an additional 10%.

All in all, the 529 plan is simply the wiser option for most families.

What to Invest In

I'm going to make this really simple so that when it comes to those sometimes-dicey, angst-filled conversations about how to invest your child's educational account you'll have nothing to wring your hands over and nothing to worry about with your spouse: Stick your educational savings in an age-based mutual fund.

That's it. That's as difficult as selecting an appropriate investment gets.

Age-based funds take into account where your child is along that continuum from gurgling infant to college-bound, high-school senior. The younger your child, the more aggressive the investments the mutual fund owns. The closer to freshman orientation at State U, the more conservative the investments. As your child grows through the years, and with you having to do precisely nothing, the mutual fund makes all the necessary incremental shifts that take the portfolio in an increasingly conservative direction. This takes the guesswork, the consternation and the discussion out of investing for college.

You'll need to check how your state handles 529 investment plans, since they often vary. Some states provide tax incentives while you're saving, others offer incentives if you use the accumulated money at an in-state school rather than on an out-of-state school. A good resource for all the necessary information you might care to know on 529 plans and other college savings options is www.savingforcollege.com. That site provides a broad overview of college savings, as well as specific information germane to each individual state.

The Pre-College Quarrels

College can be a source of tension beyond whatever financial worries you might struggle with. Often your individual backgrounds play into your personal expectations about who pays for college, causing friction between husband and wife.

I've had friends who don't fight about the need to save for college, but do fight about how much financial assistance they should offer their kids to begin with. One comes from a relatively affluent family where Mom and Dad paid every cost, from tuition to boarding to spending money. He sees the benefits in doing the same for his kids because he had no financial worries during school, graduated debt free, and saw the entire episode as a great gift from his parents. His wife came from a family that struggled to a certain degree financially, and, as a result, she had to work her way through college and had to take out a small student loan to cover what her parents weren't able to. She sees the benefits of her experience because it taught her resourcefulness as well as money- and debt-management skills that carried over into her adult life. As such, she thinks her kids would do well to carry some debt from college and work to earn part of the degree just as she did—though she and her husband can afford to pay the full expense.

This isn't really an argument about which approach is better, since each clearly has its merits. Instead, this is an argument about whose will prevails.

But imposing your will over a spouse is destructive over time. Though it won't show immediately, you are weakening the relationship's bonds. As with so many other facets of family finance, then, this is just another opportunity to build unity. And, as with all those other facets of family finance, there is no single answer that applies across the spectrum of family situations. The general framework, though, is the same as with other issues: the art of the compromise.

What can you each live with?

Would it be OK for your child to take on a little student-loan debt? What if you agree to repay the outstanding balance five years after graduation, just so your child has that experience of debt management that you find practical? If you insist on paying every penny up front, can you agree that your collegian will work to earn money for books and discretionary expenses? Numerous solutions exist, though this isn't so much about the solution as it is the process that ultimately gets you there.

It is, again, about working together as a team to achieve a financial goal in a way that you're both content with.

The Retiring Life

And you thought college was expensive.

When you're young and looking at 30 or more years of work ahead of you, the concept of retirement and its costs can be entirely foreign. And if you do grasp its importance, you know you have many, many years to get around to saving. For the time being you're preoccupied with so many other financial matters that seem so much more relevant to your life right now—living month to month on your income and wondering how you're going to save for a house, a new car, a vacation, whatever.

Take this advice to heart: Save early and save often. The future is certain to be a very expensive place, indeed.

Worse, younger couples might bear those future costs on their own. Whether or not Social Security is around, or whether it's dramatically scaled back by the time you retire is a very real concern, given the financial straits the system is in nowadays. Corporate pensions, once the primary source of retirement income you could never outlive, are pretty much gone, and those that do remain are either dying off on a regular basis or are being frozen to exclude new workers and limit what current workers are eligible to earn. The stark reality for workers under the age of 40 is that what you manage to save on your own in 401(k) plans, individual retirement accounts (IRAs), and savings and brokerage accounts will define your retirement one day. Don't save enough and you could easily run out of money in the 20 or 30 years you'll likely have in retirement. And, once again, do you really want to have to rely upon the generosity—or lack thereof—of your children to fund your golden years?

At some point, everyone who begins saving for retirement wants to know "the number"—the dollar amount they'll need to save to pay for everything up until their final breath. That number, though, doesn't exist beyond a generality—and, in general terms, you need to save an amount that's somewhere between a lot and a little more than that. The generally spouted rule of thumb is that you should save 10% of every paycheck. That's a good start, though it isn't likely to get you to where you need to be. Most of the research coming out of the financial-planning world now concludes that 15% is a more realistic number.

Either way, you have no way of predicting what your life together will cost decades from now. So many moving parts will change that number in so many expected and unexpected ways from one year to the next. You plan to raise one kid, you adopt two. Your career and income level changes. Your spouse quits work early or founds a wildly successful business. Inflation heats up. A prolonged recession sinks the stock market. A surging, multi-year bull market pushes stock prices up by unexpectedly high, double-digit gains. Where will you live? What expenses will constitute your necessary costs? How will your health hold out? Will you still be married? Heck, what are your hobbies going to be when you're 70 years old, and how much will they cost to pursue?

So many variables exist that guessing at how much it will all cost is a fairly laughable exercise. Best not to get hung up on it. Just save until you can feel it in your paycheck. If you're saving 10% and it's not affecting your budget, save 12% or 15%. If 5% is dreadfully painful, well, then, that's the number for you; don't go any higher until you can.

The ultimate size of your nest egg, though, isn't the important factor, because at the end of the day it's impossible to predict (again, you have no idea how much money you'll be able to save in the future or how your investments will perform). You will have whatever you have, and you will instinctively live within it to the best of your abilities. The important factor is simply that you purposefully saved through the years and actively planned for your retirement together.

Wanting to better tailor its products and services to the pending crush of soon-to-retire baby boomers, AIG SunAmerica, a large financial services company, surveyed thousands of retirees in the early part of the decade to get a feel for what retired life is really like. Among the various realizations was this nugget: The couples who were happiest in retirement were those who spent the longest amount of time preparing for retirement—on average, 24 years.

These retirees didn't necessarily have the most money, but they did have a far better sense of what they wanted their life in retirement to look like. Once they reached retirement, they felt better equipped to afford their chosen lifestyle, they reported being extremely satisfied with life, and were content in knowing they had the freedom to pursue whatever it is that makes their life full and rewarding.

Those who planned the shortest amount of time reported being, well, basically miserable. They were anxious about their life and uncertain if they had the resources to live as they had hoped to. Some even stated that retirement had turned out to be a nightmare.

Rhetorical question here, but which of those sounds like the retirement you're aiming for?

In Synch: What Do You Want From Retirement?

If you could design your perfect retirement before you ever reach that state of life—the vacations you want to take, the place, or places, you want to live, the hobbies or education you want to pursue, the paid or volunteer work you might like to do to stay active—how would it look?

How would your spouse answer that question? I'll bet you don't know.

Not many young couples do, because not many spend a great deal of time thinking about their combined future. There's so much life to live between now and then, and so many factors will change along the way, that it seems slightly useless to worry about your life so many years from now.

Only, it's not so useless, really. Planning is the foundation of success, whether it's planning a wedding or planning a retirement. You don't just show up at the church or chapel on the day you want to wed and expect that flowers will be in place and that a preacher, priest or rabbi will be standing there eagerly awaiting your arrival, and that all your family and friends will miraculously have congregated here at that specific time on the off chance that you decided today is the day you're getting hitched. Weddings take months of preparation for an affair that lasts just a few hours. Planning for a stage of life that will last far longer takes substantially more time.

It helps if you're both moving in a similar direction in planning your retirement. How much is life going to suck if your dream is to retire and live in a string of foreign cities for the first several years, yet your partner is expecting you two will retire to a lake house in the Ozarks? If you don't know this about each other until retirement is on your heels, you're both in for some rocky times together as you struggle with whose dream to pursue. No matter who wins, the tension will tear at the relationship, causing hurt feelings, anger and animosity that could sap a lot of the enjoyment out of retirement.

So, here's your first assignment—and it has nothing to do with money:

Grab a pencil and paper, and both of you sit down during a quiet moment and list your individual visions of retirement—your wants, needs, dreams, wishes. Whatever it is. If you think you might want it in retirement, put it on the list.

Now, compare the lists. Where does common ground exist? Where are your visions wildly divergent? This represents your first set of negotiations. What items appeal to you both? This doesn't just have to be the items you find on both lists; your list might have an item your partner really digs. Or, vice versa. That becomes a shared goal for your master list of retirement wants.

What items are important individually that you're each willing to cede to one another? Those go on the master list, as well.

What items from each other's list seem entirely unpalatable? Are you willing to drop that from your list, or is it so important that you want to negotiate for its inclusion on the master list? That might mean you have to give up something else that's important, or you have to accept something important to your partner that you're not excited about. This is a give-and-take process; remember, this isn't your life alone anymore. You're part of a team working to make both the parts— as well as the whole—as happy as possible.

Here's an example from my own life, from this very same exercise my wife and I completed several years ago. She had high on her list a desire to retire in South Louisiana, where we both grew up, a desire nowhere on my list. At the top of my list, instead, was a desire to live overseas, a dream I've had since my college days, but a dream nowhere on her list. That is potentially a vast gulf in our marriage. If I want to live overseas and she wants to live in South Louisiana, well, the commute is going to be a killer.

Yet there, fairly high on both of our lists, was the dream of spending extended time in Vancouver, Canada, a city we've visited several times and which we both love. There was a commonality we could exploit in a way that might make both of us happy: What if we save our money to buy a loft in downtown Vancouver that we can live in for several months a year? That would allow her to spend much of the year in South Louisiana, where she feels at home, and at the same time sate my dream of living abroad—in a place we both enjoy.

It's a perfect solution that suited both of us because we each end up living the retirement we want. To that end, we took the next step toward making this a reality, opening an online bank account—called The Loft Account, naturally—into which we pump a little money on occasion. One day, when we're ready and when the account is of sufficient size, we'll buy our loft in Vancouver.

Not every item need be a material pursuit. My wife, for instance, wants our budget in retirement to reflect an amount of money that will allow us to visit our two children anytime, anywhere, without causing financial hardship. Because of our backgrounds—my wife is a nurse, and I was raised by grandparents already in retirement—we both share concerns about our healthcare needs when we're older. Again, that gave us a unifying mission. When we hit 40, we researched and purchased long-term care insurance, willing to factor the cost into our monthly spending plan at a young age so that we could build into our future the peace of mind we both know we'll find comforting when we're retired.

The point is that this easy exercise revealed common ground my wife and I didn't know existed between us. It helped us map a future for our retirement that we can envision together, moving in the same direction toward a shared retirement goal. In turn, we've grown closer in our efforts at saving for retirement, because we know exactly what we want and, equally important, we know exactly what each other wants.

Now, this isn't to imply that we will get, or even pursue, everything on our list. Dreams and needs and wants change through the years as our view of life changes with age. That's expected; your only obligation to one another is to share these changing expectations as they occur so that you both remain on the same path together.

My wife and I had a positive experience, but what if there is no common ground on key wants and needs?

Let's assume for a moment that my list and my wife's list didn't include that common Vancouver tie. What would we have done, given that I want to live abroad and she wants to be in Louisiana, and there's really no middle ground there? I would have asked her to list other places she might consider living, and I would have done the same. Do any commonalities exist? And those commonalities don't have to be identical cities or states. She might have specified a desire to live by the water, and I might have noted an interest in living in a region with hills or mountains. Well, is there a place that shares both characteristics that could appeal to both of us? We do a little research online and maybe spend some vacation time over the years visiting some of these places to try the area on for size and narrow the field of possibilities that make us both happy. Or, maybe I ultimately give her Louisiana in exchange for something I really want; or she gives me overseas in exchange for something she really wants.

Compromise is the art of thinking beyond the obvious. When common ground isn't immediately apparent in your relationship, you have to expand your thinking to find the life you're both comfortable living. But take your time. You don't need a master plan for your retirement by tomorrow. You have some time to think about what you both really want.

The goal is simply to get you both moving in the same direction so that the retirement you ultimately share one day is the retirement you both want.

The 401(k) Disparity: Who Saves the Most?

Many books have been written to explain retirement-plan accounts, including my *Wall Street Journal Complete Guide to Personal Finance*, so I'm not going to offer any guidance on how to pick investments inside your 401(k) or IRA, or how much money you should be investing in each. I will only tell you that you most assuredly should be investing in your 401(k), at least to the level that you collect your company's matching contribution. That matching amount is, in the most literal sense, free money. Think about it: If your local bank promised to put 25 cents, 50 cents or even $1 into your checking account for every dollar you deposit, would you just shrug your shoulders and think "eh, no big deal?"

There is no logical reason for either spouse to let those dollars escape unless you absolutely, positively cannot afford to contribute that much without risking your ability to feed or shelter your family. If, however, you tell yourself you can't contribute up to the company match because it will crimp your lifestyle, you need to seriously reassess your rationale. Lifestyle expenses are "wants," not "needs," and if you spend your family's future financial security on appeasing your current desire to live well, your actions ultimately harm yourself and the family.

But these mechanics of retirement savings accounts are not where the matters of money and marriage generally collide (although, husbands and wives do sometimes fight about whether or not to contribute in the first place). The real marital issues more frequently evolve from disputes over who's saving how much, and the investment risks one or the other is willing to take.

Husbands and wives can get downright snippy when either feels a sense of disparity. In terms of retirement savings, this disparity can emerge in the amount of money each person is saving in a retirement plan or has already squirreled away in a retirement account. Account size matters because unlike most other types of accounts, retirement savings accounts such as a 401(k), a 403(b), a Roth IRA and others, are held only in one person's name. True, divorce laws in many states require an equal, or at least equitable distribution of retirement plan assets, and each plan has a beneficiary designation. Still, spouses often see both as somewhat hollow because in the event of divorce the beneficiary designation will likely change to a child or a future partner, and there's a great likelihood a fight will erupt over how much money an ex will get out of a retirement plan.

As such, people naturally want to feel in control of their future and want a sense of their own financial security. They want a pot of retirement dollars that they call their own. That's where the disagreements arise.

How much do each of you contribute to your individual 401(k) plan? Assuming the contributions aren't equal, the one who contributes the smaller amount, and who has the smallest account balance, is the partner who often feels shortchanged. Sometimes, this is unavoidable. A pilot marries a flight attendant; a doctor marries a nurse; a corporate executive marries a school teacher. In these situations, a sharply higher salary—and possibly benefits such as an annual bonus automatically deposited into a retirement account—naturally creates inequality. Other times, selfishness is at play. The family can only afford to save so much money each month, and the spouse in charge of budgeting consciously saves a larger portion of those investment dollars in his or her retirement account, leaving the other able to save a much smaller sum.

Neither situation is particularly fair, though one is much less fair than the other. The key to successfully managing the disparity starts in acknowledging that it exists and addressing whatever feelings it engenders. And if one partner is feeling shortchanged, solutions can be relatively simple.

The simplest of all: Accept the fact that the partner saving the smallest amount has a legitimate need and desire to save more money, and let that spouse save more money, even if that means the one saving the most has to scale back a bit. Remember, 401(k) contributions reduce your take-home pay, so if one of you starts saving more, that will necessarily impact your budget. If that added savings reduces your discretionary income, fine; that's just a few restaurant meals you skip each month. But if saving more would eat into fixed costs, then the spouse currently saving the most will have to trim back to allow necessary room in the budget. The family will still be saving the same amount of money, just in more equitable fashion. (A caveat here: If one partner's plan awards matching contributions of, say, $1 on all money saved up to 7% of salary, and the other's plan awards 50 cents on all savings up to 3%, then it generally makes more sense to meet the matching contributions of that first plan, since the amount of free money available is greater. But this is only the case if the differentials are noticeably wide. If your plan pays 50 cents on the first 5%, and your partner's pays 50 cents on the first 3%, well, there's not a huge spread involved, so stick to the equitable distribution.)

There are two ways to define equality: You both save the same dollar amount each year, or the same percentage. Saving the same dollar amount is self-explanatory. If you determine together that the budget can stand to have $12,000 a year go into retirement savings, then you both save $6,000, though for one that might be 6% of salary and 9% for the other.

Saving the same percentage amount, meanwhile, means you will be saving different sums, depending upon salary differences. This arrangement tends to work best in relationships where two salaries are relatively similar; that way neither of you feels slighted that your partner is saving more. Let's say you agree that each of you can save 10% of your salary. If one earns $100,000 annually, and the other earns $50,000, then simple math tells you that one of you will be saving $10,000 and the other $5,000 a year. That can be problematic for some people, though others won't care. Moreover, there's nothing inherently wrong with this approach. That's just the benefit the highest earner gets for having achieved a higher pay scale.

Fact is, you enter into marriage assuming you'll be together until the end, and every day you work at making that a reality. And when retirement arrives, the location of the money you two will live on is fairly pointless. It's not like your dollars are only going to pay for your expenses, to heck with your partner. All the money that comes into the relationship is money for the relationship, regardless of origin.

Nevertheless, be aware of the fact that frustrations over retirement savings accounts can simmer out of sight when one partner is saving more than the other. There is sometimes an unspoken need to feel equal. Address it and you erase the tension—and it costs you nothing to do so, since generally the same number of dollars will end up headed into retirement accounts.

Risk Management

This is potentially a more inflammatory issue among couples than the amount of money going into individual retirement accounts. Risk is an intensely personal, emotional matter, both sides of which can seem entirely foreign to partners in a marriage. Where one sees an acceptable trade off between risk and potential reward, the other sees an unmitigated disaster looming over the family like a piano hanging by a thread. Likewise, where one sees safety and security, the other sees family money completely neutered by an unnatural aversion to acceptable investment risk.

This is a really simplistic way of getting at this divide, but figure out where you fall along the spectrum between the two extremes above, asking yourself and your spouse this question and choosing one of the answers:

What is my primary interest in investing?

a. To achieve high rates of return over the long term, even if that requires tolerating substantial swings in the value of my portfolio over short-term periods.

b. To maintain stable growth in the value of my portfolio through turbulent periods, even if it means lower returns over the longer term.

c. To minimize fluctuations in value while maximizing long-term returns.

There's no need to explain what it means if you choose one answer over the other. The personality differences are self-evident in the answers, and they clearly identify the potential challenges that exist if one of you selects A and the other opts for B.

You goal is to reach answer C together. That doesn't mean you both have to forsake your way of thinking. It just means that you both have to create an approach to managing the family's money in a manner that makes you both feel content.

Let's first look at the conflict. In purely clinical terms, risk is simply the variability of returns of a particular investment, meaning it is the up and down swings that naturally occur in every investment market. You cannot control these; no one can. Like money itself, investment risk is neither good nor bad because you can profit from both up and down movements. The problem is our perception of risk, our fear that everything we've staked on some venture will evaporate and that we will then feel bad about having lost all this money.

Risk is a highly individualistic emotion. Perfect example: My wife and I spent a long weekend in Las Vegas in November 2007. While I played with several hundred dollars at the craps table, wagering between $30 and $150 at any given moment, she was at a nearby slot machine nearly hyperventilating, she told me back in the hotel room, because she realized after a few spins that she had accidentally wagered 50 cents per turn instead of the 25 cents she had previously been betting. She was only willing to gamble $10 at a time, and this quarter-sized mistake was depleting her asset much too rapidly for her comfort. This is, I guarantee, an entirely true account—she was upset at risking an extra 25 cents when I was throwing down hundreds of dollars. She thought I was nuts; I thought she was too much of a financial teetotaler. But it's all in your perspective. After all, the guy wagering on the dice right next to me arrived at the table with $11,000, well past the crazy zone by my standards, though I'm certain my relatively meager stake was as penny-ante to him as my wife's 25-cent slot pulls were to me.

That's how risk manifests itself inside our heads, a concept you have to understand in order to effectively manage the matter inside a marriage. You cannot suppose that your tolerance for risk defines how the family will invest. Impose your acceptance of high-octane risk in pursuit of a higher level of returns and you potentially create an unnecessary level of internal worry and stress for your partner, though your partner might not display that outwardly. Conversely, impose your intolerance for any risk and shuttle the family's money into riskless bank accounts, certificates of deposit and government bonds, and you potentially create a similar backlash in a spouse who is uncomfortable with the idea that the family's wealth is not working as hard as it should to grow larger over time.

This is a situation where respect is the key factor. You each must respect that your spouse has a different view than you do and that those feelings are just as legitimate as yours. Fear of loss—the heart of the emotional side of risk—is a powerful stimulant, and in this case "loss" can be the actual loss of money from an investment gone bad, or the loss of earning power from money inappropriately invested.

Part of the solution here is investment education. Researchers from the University of Central Florida studied how gender relates to risk-taking among mutual-fund investors and found that, generally speaking, women are more risk-averse than men. However, that aversion shrinks dramatically as investment knowledge improves. The take-away: Partners who help their spouse learn about investing can reduce a great deal of the tension that stems from divergent assessments of risk.

The other part of success comes in negotiating a middle ground, a place where you are both comfortable with the overall portfolio of investments the family owns, from basic certificates of deposit to far riskier stocks and mutual funds. You can accomplish a lot of this through the investment accounts you both own, building each account individually but with an eye toward how they work in concert. What I mean is this: If you happen to be the one comfortable with risk, then maybe you overload your accounts with the riskier assets. Your partner's account, meanwhile, would be built largely from less-risky assets. On an individual basis, your partner is content with an account that is clearly built to survive the vicissitudes of the market, while you're content to aim for the higher returns over the longer haul. Yet the combined effect is a prudently balanced family portfolio built for growth and stability.

If you can't manage any of this on your own—meaning you make no progress toward middle ground—consider spending some time together with a financial planner. A good planner who charges by the hour or as a percentage of the assets under management—as opposed to one focused on selling products for a commission—will serve as a neutral third party capable of helping you build a portfolio that appeals to you both.

Estate Planning: Preparing for the Inevitable

Young couples in particular often overlook this piece of their financial life because, well, you're young and you're never going to die. Many also wrongly believe that they have no estate to begin with, so why plan for one.

Why? Well, if you don't plan for your estate—and if you have a single asset as simple as a checking account, you have an estate—the state will plan it for you, and the state won't necessarily distribute your assets the way you want.

What people generally don't see is that having no estate plan in place means leaving a potentially devastating void in your family's life. The untimely, unexpected death of a young spouse—and "young" could mean your twenties, thirties or forties—can have ruinous repercussions on a surviving spouse and their children. What would be the impact on your family's financial situation if you die?

What about if your partner dies? Could you alone afford the family's cost of living? The cost of college?

What happens if you and your spouse die? Who gets your assets? Who raises your children, assuming you have kids or plan to have kids?

These are not hypothetical questions. Bad things happen to good families. My train into New York City from New Jersey was ten minutes late the morning of September 11, 2001; otherwise I would have been in the basement of the World Trade Center exiting a subway car just about the time the terrorist attacks occurred. That event finally forced me to confront the need for life insurance and a will, estate planning fundamentals that I had disregarded for years simply because pursuing either felt a little creepy, like I was conceding my mortality and telegraphing to the gods of fate that it was OK to kill me now. But I think about what might have been: My wife would have struggled to pay the mortgage and our son's elementary school tuition on her salary alone, likely forcing her to downscale their life. Years later she would have to struggle to afford his college costs, which we hope to cover to some degree. And all that would be on top of the incredible emotional impact of losing a husband, and the father of her child.

Moments like that make you realize just how vulnerable families are to financial disaster. An unexpected tragedy arrives to alter your life irrevocably. The tragedy itself is bad enough, but then comes the financial impact to magnify the pain. Preparation can at least make the aftermath less traumatic financially.

Life Insurance: Who and What to Insure

Insurance just sounds boring. And, really, it is. Nothing terribly exciting about it at all. Nevertheless, insurance is one of life's necessities that rounds out your financial security. So, prepare to be bored . . .

When you're single, you do not need life insurance—unless you have a child or other dependents who rely on your income in some manner. In that case, you want to insure your life and your ability to earn income in the event you one day can't provide for them, either because of your death or disability.

When you're married, you may not need insurance either. If, for example, you and your spouse work, then your death wouldn't prevent your spouse from earning a living. In that case, there's no screaming demand for life insurance, though you might carry a small policy of $10,000 or $20,000 to pay for funeral expenses, since dying can be such a costly thing to do.

The moment you absolutely, positively need life insurance is the minute a child enters your life. Suddenly, your financial obligations shift in profound ways. Now, your death or disability could fundamentally impact your child's current and future life, from housing to education. You need to insure against that possibility, and that's exactly the role life insurance plays—it insures against the loss of your greatest asset: your ability to earn an income.

In simplest terms, life insurance pays a lump sum of money to your beneficiary in the event you die during the coverage period. That period can cover your entire lifetime or a pre-determined number of years, such as, say, 10 or 20 years. Life insurance comes in a variety of flavors, but essentially it boils down to so-called term life and permanent life.

- **Term life policies remain in force for a specified term—that is, 20 years.** If you die within the coverage period, you win—so to speak: Your beneficiary receives a check for the full amount of the coverage. If you die after the policy's term expires, well you lose twice—not only are you dead, but your beneficiary receives nothing.

- **Permanent life insurance hangs around forever.** So long as you pay the premiums, your beneficiary receives the payout when you die. Unlike term life, permanent life usually comes packaged with what is effectively a savings/investment account that grows larger through the years based on some investment formula built into the policy. That so-called cash value is money that, at some point, you can borrow against or use to pay the premiums on the policy itself.

The question you face, then, is whether you want a straightforward death benefit or a death benefit with a built-in savings account. Yes, the latter sounds more appealing because you're building up cash value that you can use one day. But that cash value comes at a steep price—namely, the price of the policy.

Generally speaking, Permanent life policies are meaningfully more expensive than term life policies offering the same dollar amount of coverage. Term life coverage that costs several hundred dollars a year will, for the same amount of coverage, cost several thousand as a permanent life policy, depending on the policy. For that reason, term life is generally the better buy. You can effectively buy far more coverage at a far more affordable price. Instances certainly exist where you might consider a permanent life policy, but they are generally complex estate-planning reasons that you probably don't have to fret with as a relatively young couple. For younger newlyweds, a term life policy that adequately covers your obligations to house and educate your children is the place to start.

How much coverage you need depends entirely on your income and the amount of assets you already have accumulated that could be used, if needed, by a surviving spouse. The rule of thumb says you need a policy that provides five to seven times your salary. But your situation could be sharply different. If, for instance, you have no mortgage, or your child's educational costs are already covered by a trust funded by your parents, then your insurance needs are substantially different. This is where you need to talk to a fee-only financial planner or a trusted insurance agent who you are comfortably sure isn't just trying to sell you any old policy to generate the commission.

And whatever you do, stick to reputable insurers—those that carry high ratings of A or better from the ratings agencies like Moody's, Fitch and Standard & Poor's. This is a financial product that will stick with you for decades; you want to know that your insurer is strong enough financially to stick around with you as well, and will have the finances necessary to pay the claim if necessary. In practical terms that means you should not simply choose the cheapest policy because it's cheap. Look for a combination of affordability and financial might.

One last note about insurance: Lots of couples pursue a single-income existence, typically with Mom staying at home with the kids while Dad earns the income. In that situation, the couple will insure Dad's life to protect that income, but skip out on insuring Mom's life since she earns no income. Resist that urge. That's a financial catastrophe in waiting.

What makes you assume Dad would be fine financially if Mom dies? She's providing a variety of services for which Dad will suddenly be on the hook: transportation to and from school; childcare before and after work; transportation to and from extracurricular events; management of doctor appoints and transportation there and back; shopping; cooking; cleaning. There's also the potential earnings that Mom represents in the event she could have returned to the workforce to help afford college or other expenses.

To protect the family appropriately, carry insurance on a non-working spouse in instances where the family has kids. This will prevent many sleepless nights for the surviving spouse.

Wills

After life insurance, a will is the foundation of estate planning. It's the playbook for how every asset you own—from money to gold jewelry to baseball cards—is divvied up. Even if you're single a will is a smart document to have since you might have specific bequests you'd like to make that your estate wouldn't necessarily make after your death without explicit instructions left by you. You might, for instance, want to leave a particular asset to a niece or nephew or friend; that won't happen without a will because no one knows your intentions unless they're written, signed and witnessed.

Couples in particular absolutely need wills. Without a will, you die "intestate," arguably one of the more selfish financial acts. The reason: Dying intestate leaves your spouse with potentially hefty and unnecessary costs and tax consequences that you could have lessened or avoided had you chosen to write a will. Worse, the state generally determines where the assets go and in what allocation. Those rules vary by state, but you can pretty much assure that the state probably isn't going to divide your assets the way you'd divide them.

Just because you write a will once doesn't mean you're all set. Wills are living documents in that they can be amended an unlimited number of times while you're alive—and they should be. Your life changes through the years as assets come and go. The number of kids you have can change. You may divorce your spouse. All are situations that will require you to redraw your will.

You can find all manner of do-it-yourself will-writing programs online these days, some better than others. Nolo.com is one of the better providers of legal documents written in plain English that are easy for everyday consumers to navigate. Just be aware that some do-it-yourself legal documents aren't recognized by some states, or are not built to deal with complicated estate-planning issues. If you have a simple estate and simple directives in your will, a do-it-yourself kit can work fine. But if any complexity exists, stick with a pro who's an expert in estate-planning law. This is one area where an unintentional screw up can negate your will, send your assets in unintended directions and cause undue headaches for survivors.

For couples with children, you want to ensure that your will names a guardian to raise your kids and a trustee to manage the money and assets you leave behind for them. This is perhaps where the greatest potential for conflict emerges. Not all couples instantly agree on who should raise their children if they both were to die. You might not get along with your in-laws, or maybe your spouse isn't a fan of your parents or siblings. How do you work that out when it's likely each of you will choose your own family members as guardians? And what if either set of grandparents is a clear choice, but both are up in age—is it fair to impose parenthood on them at this stage of life? Is it fair to your children?

Maybe you know a sibling or a friend would be the greatest parent imaginable to your children. But what if this sibling or friend already has several children? Is it fair to that person to make them responsible—both emotionally and financially—for another child, and is it fair to put your child in a situation where the competition for affection and resources is already possibly strained?

As with so many facets of family finance, there cannot be a single answer that covers every family situation. But there is a tool you can use to help you identify the guardian who might best serve that role for your children: the interview process.

Make a short list of contenders, those that you both agree on as well as those that only one of you feels strongly about. Then interview them. Tell them to imagine that you died yesterday and that they need to take your kids starting today. How, you want to know, would they handle the change to their life, and how would they raise your child?

Don't think in overarching terms, you want to know the details. What will the would-be guardians do about bedrooms and the potential need for more space? Are they planning more kids of their own and how would that impact what they're able to provide your child or children? How will they handle a situation in which your aspirations for your child, and the available funding you leave behind, exceed what they had planned or are capable of affording for their own child? What if that situation is reversed? How do they handle those instances, since both potentially create haves and have-nots within the same family?

Their answers and attitude will say a lot about whether they consider your request a privilege or a burden—or, in financial terms, an investment or an expense. You obviously want the guardian who sees raising your child as a privilege, and you might be surprised at which family it is that gives that impression. So be open to candidates you might not have high on your list.

Other Legal Documents

Power-of-Attorney

This can be very handy for couples, particularly in situations where one of you needs to act on behalf of the other in an emergency or when one of you is incapacitated. This document can allow for all sorts of activities, such as managing investments held individually, signing tax returns, selling off property or even accessing a safe-deposit box that, for whatever reason, is titled only in one person's name.

Powers-of-attorney are also useful in situations when you and your spouse are traveling together and a temporary guardian, such as an in-law, is watching over your children. This short-term power-of-attorney will allow the guardian to act on your behalf as it relates to your child's welfare.

Trusts

These are typically used inside a marriage to protect assets for children. You can arrange trusts in a variety of ways. Some trusts you'll fund while you're still alive, setting aside money for a child's education that you want to ensure will not be corrupted by a divorce, creditors or any potential lawsuit. In other cases, a trust will form only on your death, and will be funded by the assets you bequeath to it in your will.

A trustee who you name—and that can be a family member, a trusted friend, a lawyer or a bank trust department, among others—will manage the assets in the trust to your specifications. You can determine when this trust will begin to distribute assets and under what conditions, or under what conditions it won't distribute assets.

Testamentary Letters

These types of letters are similar to a will but are generally handwritten and limited to items of smaller value, such as family keepsakes that have sentimental meaning. This could be non-collectible art, dishes and heirlooms that have been in the family for a generation or more, baseball cards, a coin collection, furniture and so forth. While states generally accept a testamentary letter as legally binding, you might still want to have someone such as a notary public witness your signature. Also, make references to your testamentary letter in your will, so that beneficiaries and executors know it exists.

What Documents to Keep Where

Over time, we all collect an assortment of important or semi-important papers and keepsakes. Our inclination often is to stick these documents and doodads in a safe-deposit box at the bank or maybe a fireproof lockbox you hide in the closet somewhere. But different documents demand storage in different locations, otherwise you can create potential headaches for yourself. Some documents you don't need to keep to begin with.

So, you need to know what to keep and where to keep it.

A safe-deposit box is good place to keep many documents because of its safety, but that safety means little if you need access to the box at hours when the bank is closed. Moreover, the people you designate to handle your affairs if you die or become incapacitated may not have access to the box until a lawyer files all the appropriate paperwork, and that can cause potential problems for heirs and survivors.

Basically, you want to split your documents into those you keep at home in a lockbox, and those stored in a bank's safe-deposit box.

Lockbox Docs:

- Wills
- Trusts
- Powers-of-attorney
- Burial insurance policy
- Social Security cards
- Passports

In the event of your death or incapacity, family members and representatives of your estate will need access to these documents quickly, and emergencies don't necessarily happen during banking hours. Just be sure that someone in the family aside from you and your spouse knows where the lockbox is located, how to access it and what they'll find inside that they might need.

The passport, by the way, isn't an emergency document, but you never know

What Documents to Keep Where, continued

when you're going to do something goofy like lose your wallet and need proof of your identity for a variety of reasons—and you won't want to have your passport locked up in a safe-deposit box for a few days until the bank opens.

It's a good idea to also keep in the lockbox all your life-insurance policy numbers and contact information. The insurers won't need the contract itself to begin processing a claim but they will need the policy number, so make it convenient for those assigned to manage your affairs.

Safe-Deposit Box Docs:

- Birth and death certificates
- Marriage certificates and divorce decrees
- Adoption and custody papers
- Baptismal/religious records
- Military records
- Citizenship/naturalization papers
- Property deeds
- Vehicle titles
- Any financial securities, such as stocks and bonds, that aren't kept by your brokerage firm
- Home improvement records—usually receipts—that help determine the cost-basis of your home for tax reasons

All of these are documents that you won't likely need quickly, but they're documents not easily replaced, or that can take weeks or months to replace—and you might not have that kind of time to wait.

While you store the originals in the safe-deposit box, keep a copy in the lockbox at home that you or family members can reference as needed.

Finally, keep a "go-kit" somewhere easily and immediately accessible so that in the event of a emergency that drives you out of your home—think hurricanes, wildfires and other such disasters—you can quickly grab a copy of every important document you will need to put your life back on track.

This go-kit should contain copies of:

- All your various insurance policies
- Every family member's birth certificate
- Family Social Security cards
- Passports
- Driver's licenses
- An inventory of household goods, with photos (so that if the house is destroyed, you have photographic evidence to show the insurance company. Keep the photos on a thumb-sized computer drive to save space)
- Emergency contact numbers for family, friends, neighbors, physicians, insurance companies and local remodelers (handy for getting a quick jump on home repairs that may be needed after a disaster)
- Bank account numbers and bank branch phone numbers
- Keep these documents in a waterproof bag, stored in a portable, fireproof lockbox that you can grab in an emergency. In the aftermath of a disaster, these documents can help you get your life back on track much more quickly.

Everything I Know You Should Know, Too

How much do you know about the family's finances? Where, for instance, are all the financial accounts located? How much money do they hold? If your spouse dies or falls gravely ill, do you know how to access the accounts online or which institutions to visit to reclaim your assets? What about insurance policies? The keys to the safe-deposit box? Do you even know if you two have a safe-deposit box . . . or what's in it?

Now, how much of this does your spouse know?

If what you know about the family's financial life and what your spouse knows are not equal, you've got a problem. All manner of potential pitfalls are lurking in the darkness. The most obvious is that situation where the partner who knows everything dies and the partner who knows little is left groping for answers to where all the money, assets, policies and legal documents are located. In such a case, some accounts might be lost forever if the survivor doesn't know to look for them.

Less dramatic is the situation in which the partner who knows little about the family's money ends up feeling financially disenfranchised. This clueless partner might be worried that the family isn't progressing financially or that decisions are being made unilaterally, leading to a growing sense of unease and annoyance.

In many instances these circumstances arise from oversight. The spouse who controls the money doesn't think to include a partner who has shown no prior inclination to balance accounts, pick investments or even ask about that stuff. In some cases it's blissful ignorance as one spouse purposefully cedes control over the numbingly mundane and sometimes abstruse logistics of dollars-and-cents minutia. In some instances, the reason is much more malevolent—a partner is using money as a tool of oppression, keeping a spouse financially weakened and dependent.

None of these situations is ideal, and the last one—the overt malevolence—is intolerable. Every couple needs equal knowledge of what the family owns and where it is. This doesn't imply you, the blissfully ignorant one, must take control of the money. You don't have to make financial decisions. The family doesn't need a power-sharing arrangement. You don't even have to pay attention to the accounts more than a few times a year, and even then only for a few, brief moments. But, for your own sense of financial security, you both need to know what exists and where, and for some very good reasons:

Reason #1

Something seriously bad befalls the spouse who controls the money, such as a death or a mentally debilitating injury, and the surviving partner is left to pick up the finances, unaware, however, that there is a certificate of deposit at First National Bank across town; a brokerage account online that requires an unknown password; and a home equity line of credit at Second National Bank that can be tapped in an emergency (such as this). There's a life/disability insurance policy the injured spouse has at work, but you don't know about that, and an individual retirement account at a mutual fund company you've never heard of. The list goes on.

Sure, you'll find out about these accounts in due time, when the statements or bills roll in. But that could be weeks or months after you really need to know about them, when earlier knowledge could have eased your angst. Some accounts might go undetected for years, or become lost entirely.

It is so much smarter in this situation, so much less traumatic, to know where all the assets are from the outset so that the surviving partner can access them quickly, if needed.

Reason #2

You wake up one morning—or come home one evening—to find your finances in shambles. You're up to your nose in debt about which you were clueless, the retirement savings you thought you had is now a goose egg, your head is spinning from your spouse talking about the need to file bankruptcy and you're still trying to get your head around the idea that MasterCard claims you owe $40,000 for charges you've never seen. Oh, and, honey, the house is in foreclosure so we have to move to a new place quickly.

I know that sounds utterly contrived, but this sort of unwelcome moment—the complete unraveling of all that you know as normal in your life—is more common that you think. Spouses who cede control of the family finances and blithely go about life in blissful monetary ignorance often find out much too late that in doing so they effectively destroyed their own lives.

Love is built on trust. That's great. So, go ahead and trust your spouse . . . but verify.

If only for financial self-preservation reasons you must know everything your spouse knows. That way you are intimately familiar with all the assets and all the liabilities. Yes, there are ways to hide both, but we'll get to that in a minute.

Reason #3

Nothing bad happens to either of you. But you're feeling a sense of financial insecurity because from what you can see, the family really isn't getting ahead. The stagnant savings account down at the bank has seemed lifeless, stuck at the same level forever, and from what you can see in the checkbook, money comes in and money goes out and your financial life seems moribund after all these years together.

Only, what you don't know is that the 401(k) plan has a ton of money in it, the IRA is looking pretty healthy, too, and there's an online savings account you never pay attention to that has a year's worth of salary stuffed into it. Your spouse knows all that, however, having been the one to arrange and fund all these accounts over the years. If only you knew about this you'd be swaddled in a sense of financial contentedness, recognizing that your present is secure and your future's looking bright. And you'd never have to worry with this again.

The only way to reach that point: Keep up with the finances, even if that means just taking a peek from time to time to remind yourself about everything the family owns.

Both partners have their own responsibilities in addressing Reasons 1, 2 and 3.

In very general terms, two types of relationships exist when it comes to how couples manage finances: the gatekeeper marriage and the marriage of equals. Each has its own requirements when it comes you and your partner's obligations to one another—and yourself.

The Gatekeeper Marriage

In relationships where one spouse controls the finances, that gatekeeper is obligated to produce two reports: a family account list and an account value statement.

FAMILY ACCOUNT LIST

Just what it sounds like—a detailed list of every account, replete with account number, institution name and location, online access data including login and password information, physical address of the institution and a contact name and phone number (if applicable), and the location where the necessary documents are stored (this might be a file-cabinet in the house, a family safe, a bank safe-deposit box or the family's attorney, financial planner or CPA). This list is updated whenever accounts are added or deleted, or relevant account information changes, such as passwords.

ACCOUNT VALUATION STATEMENT

This is the individual value of each account. A simple spreadsheet with each account listed will suffice. The statement should be updated quarterly, at the very least, or whenever the partner not in control of the finances requests a new report.

And speaking of the partner who cedes financial control . . . your obligation is to peruse the reports when you receive them, and ask questions if you have them, such as, "What is the new account? I've never seen it before. Is my name on there as a joint owner?" Keep the account list and the valuation statements handy, though certainly in a secure place, given the nature of the data contained in each. Pay attention to trends. If you remember that the savings account held $45,000 the last time you saw one of these reports, and it now has just $12,000, ask where the money went. It could be a legitimate reason, like your partner transferring money into the joint brokerage account, or some such rationale.

On occasion, double check the authenticity of the data. Log in to websites to see if the balances match up. Ask to see the bank statements or other documents that come into the house. Again, love all you want. But trust and verify.

The Marriage of Equals

In relationships where you share the financial duties, you're each going to know a lot about your specific areas, but might know little about the areas your spouse is handling. In this case, come together once a quarter to build the exact same family account list and account valuation statement. It might take you part of an afternoon one weekend to build the initial lists, but after that the quarterly follow-up will only take a few minutes for each of you to fill in the necessary blanks, or to add new accounts or delete the defunct accounts.

Now, regardless of which arrangement you use—the gatekeeper or marriage of equals—you might find yourself wondering one day: How do I know my partner isn't hiding assets or debts somewhere? There are a couple ways to figure this out.

As I mentioned in Section One, you should each be examining one another's credit report on an annual basis, or at least every few years. Hiding any debt is absolutely impossible unless your spouse owes gambling debts to Vinny the Bookie or has been borrowing from sketchy loan sharks. Because debt follows you like a shadow, it will show up on a credit report.

Unknown credit cards are the primary debt accounts you're looking for, since they can be obtained individually. But don't overlook other possibilities. I know a man whose wife approached a local banker with whom they were close friends, and obtained a home-equity line of credit without telling her husband. Imagine the husband's surprise when the banker casually mentioned the line of credit one day. Imagine his horror and anger when he realized his wife had drawn down a huge portion of the account for a shopping addiction. She is now his ex-wife.

Every year you can download at www.annualcreditreport.com a free copy of your credit report from each of the three leading reporting agencies. Do so, and share the reports with one another.

Hiding assets is easier, and people who are determined to do so will find a way to secret away precious metals or cash, or open financial accounts overseas. The best you can generally do is pay attention to the mail. Specifically, look for what appear to be financial-oriented envelopes, particularly if the names aren't familiar.

Pay attention as well to the annual tax return. In most families, one spouse will gather the documents and either prepare the taxes personally or ship everything to a tax pro. The other spouse just signs the tax return and that's that. Scan the numbers instead, paying particular attention to the first page, where all the income is denoted. Based on what you know you and your spouse earn, and based on whatever dividend and interest income is listed, does the cumulative income seem accurate? Assets are easier to hide than debt, but if the money is in any account that generates any level of income, a tax document is produced somewhere, and that will show up on the tax return. If you file taxes separately, both of you must share your returns with the other.

At the end of the day, the goal is simply to be aware of your financial surroundings. And that means that even if you abhor the notion of reading a tax return or a brokerage statement, you have to at least take a few moments from your life occasionally to know where your family's assets are located and how you can access them. You might need that information in an emergency one day.

Conclusion

Way back in the early pages of this book, back amid those questions to ask before you marry someone, I noted that my wife and I had tried several different approaches to managing our daily finances through the years. Well, let me tell you the whole story . . .

When we first married, in 1992, we dutifully opened a joint checking account at what was then First Interstate Bank in Southern California, where we lived at the time. It was an unmitigated disaster, we both agree. I never paid attention to the checkbook because I used a credit card for everything. She rarely used a credit card, instead writing checks for every purchase. Each month we struggled to understand why our finances were so screwed up; we never had enough money to go around because I was freely spending on the credit card, not knowing what she was spending out of the checkbook. And because she would look in the checkbook and see that I wasn't writing any checks, she just assumed we had all that money available to buy whatever she needed to buy.

When the credit card bills arrived, the façade crumbled. And we argued and grumbled about each other's profligate ways.

So, we decided the best bet was to separate. Not matrimonially, financially. We both headed to the same First Interstate branch and opened individual checking accounts. We kept the joint account to pay joint bills, but we paid each other an allowance from our paychecks that went into our individual accounts that we could use however we wanted. We even had individual credit cards. And all was generally well; no real financial arguments except under-the-breath commentary about some stupid purchases we saw each other wasting money on.

A few years passed and by this time we were living in Dallas, where we had our accounts at what was then NationsBank. But to keep the accounts from charging us monthly fees, we had to have savings accounts, each loaded with $1,500, that were tied back to our individual checking accounts as well as the joint account. The net effect: my wife and I, just two people, had six checking and savings accounts between us. My paycheck was being directly deposited into my individual account, while my wife deposited her paper-based paycheck into the joint account and wrote herself a check to then deposit into her individual account. Then, every month, we had six accounts to balance and reconcile. We had reached the epitome of financial complication, and we both realized that separate but equal was no way to live your financial life inside a marriage.

We renewed our vows financially, so to speak, by reuniting all of our assets into a single joint checking account and single joint money-market account.

In doing so, we implicitly accepted a set of rules we knew to be inviolable. We could not spend wantonly from the joint accounts, knowing that the other may have expenses to manage, too. We had to talk to one another about relatively big expenses we were considering, since we both had to agree on the amount of money coming out of the account. We had to find a unified way of managing the credit cards and checkbook so that we didn't end up in the same situation we fell into in the early years of marriage.

In short: We had to communicate. And we had to be wide open about our finances, since anything that was hidden, we knew, would erupt like a lanced boil.

We've operated this way now for the better part of a decade. And we've never had a problem, except for a time or three with miscalculating the additions and subtractions in the register while balancing the checkbook. In the process, we have become far better stewards of our money because we're managing it together, both seeing exactly what is coming and going through our financial life. Because of that, we've been able to steer more of our dollars into our version of financial security, which, for us, is a fatter bank account, larger retirement accounts, savings for our kids' future and a retirement home on a lake that we bought well before retirement so that we could begin building memories there together and with our children.

Perhaps best of all, we've all but eradicated arguments. We certainly still disagree over certain expenses we each want to make—every family is like that—but I can't think of the last time we've fought about money, about one of us controlling the purse strings or spending so much that the other is angry or where there's not enough money in the checking account to pay the bill. We simply don't fight about money.

We have, in effect, matured financially. It took some time to get here. And it took a lot of communication and learning exactly how to talk to one another. But that's the power of words. Everything you need to succeed financially as newlyweds rests in your larynx and your head. You only need to learn to express yourself in ways that don't incite anger, that aren't belittling and that aren't hurtful. Talking will do so much more for you than silence. You need to learn to analyze and manage your emotions, and understand that your partner's emotions may not necessarily reflect yours—and that there's nothing wrong with that because everyone is different, and everyone was raised with different experiences with money.

Marriage is the hardest job you'll ever have—at least until kids come along. Money shouldn't be the issue you argue about most or that causes you both the most stress. And it doesn't have to be if you practice all that I've laid out in the previous pages. If you're unsure of how to talk to one another about money just yet, write an e-mail. If you hate writing e-mails, use the phone. If you're clueless about the money you and your spouse have or where all the accounts and documents are, you have to learn to speak up for yourself. If you know your spouse is in that position, you have to learn to open up. If you can't figure out where you money goes, track your spending more closely, then build a budget together and stick to it. Another brief example from my life: My wife and I have determined that we have a set number of dollars that we can spend every week on extraneous purchases like restaurant meals or new shoes or, in my case, a new soccer ball. We keep it in an envelope in our basket of monthly bills, and extract the money as needed. If either of us uses a credit card instead of cash to buy something spontaneously, we take the money from the envelope and put it back into the bank so that it's there to pay the credit card. It's the way we have determined works best for our family, and it keeps us within the framework of the budget we laid out together. Again, it forces us to interact financially so that we stick to the path we've outlined so that we can reach other joint and individual goals.

In the end, that's what keeps financial flare-ups from ever igniting. If you're both getting what you want out of your money, if you both feel a sense of financial security, if you both feel financially equal, and if you're both openly communicating about your financial needs and the money that flows through your life, you will have very little to fight over when it comes to money.

And if there's no financial conflict, then there's no way money can tear your relationship asunder.

Index